Civil War Weapons

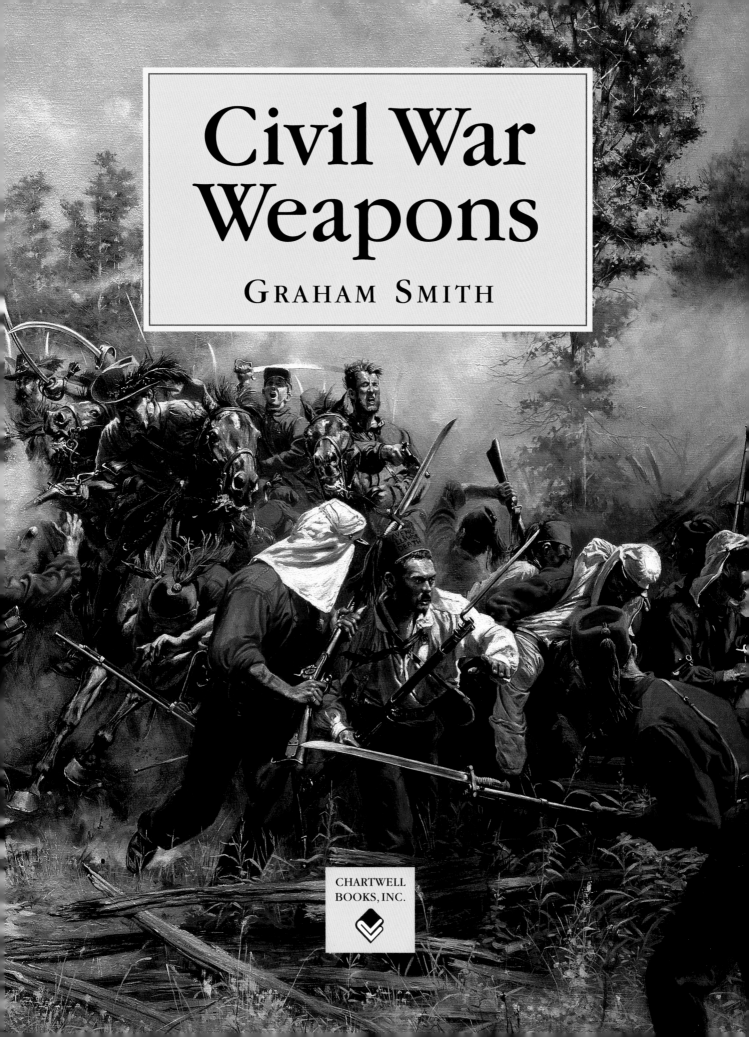

Civil War
Weapons

Graham Smith

CHARTWELL
BOOKS, INC.

Copyright ©2011 Pepperbox Press Ltd.

This edition published in 2011 by
CHARTWELL BOOKS, INC.
A division of BOOK SALES, INC.
276 Fifth Avenue Suite 206
New York, New York 10001
USA

ISBN-13: 978-0-7858-2854-9

Printed in China

Contents

WARMAN'S CIVIL WAR WEAPONS

Introduction

From the first cannon shots fired at Fort Sumter, Charleston, on April 12, 1861, the fighting men of the Union and the Confederate States fought each other with determination, courage and conviction. And by the time of the last Confederate surrenders in May 1865, the fighting had ranged over huge areas of the country, on mountain, plain, forest, city and river.

The statistics are staggering. In four years of war, nearly 3 million men fought on both sides and over 620,000 of them died. Countless others were left maimed and ruined by illness, disease and their wounds. What's more, these numbers don't take into account the civilians who suffered from disease, starvation and destruction as the warring armies swept back and forth. And all this amongst a population of only 32 million. More Americans died in the Civil War than in all America's other wars combined, and if the same proportions applied to a conflict today it would mean over *5 million* deaths. A true national cataclysm, the war was the defining moment in the nation's history.

So when the farm boys, clerks, lawyers, doctors, artisans and laborers of both sides enthusiastically flocked to their colors, what tools were they given? As the pages of this book make clear, a bewildering array of weapons found their way into the hands of the fighting men. When the war began, the armories of the tiny United States military held a mixture of obsolete and current government equipment, and were quickly emptied by both sides. But this wasn't nearly enough to equip the newly raised formations. Many men brought their own weapons, perhaps a pistol, revolver or shotgun, or for the wealthy maybe a fine hunting rifle or a high-quality sword. Shortages of firearms were so great in the early days of the war that some men even trained with pikes and lances.

Existing arsenals increased production as fast as they could, while contracts for government pattern weapons were awarded to enterprising private businessmen. Purchasing agents travelled the world looking for weapons, some of which were the equal to anything produced in America, while others were obsolete stocks unloaded at a good price by unscrupulous governments and companies.

War is also a driver for technological change, and as can be seen in the following pages, the Civil War was responsible for dramatic developments in weapons design. Engineers and gunmakers came up with new concepts, some of which were of more danger to the user than the enemy. Others went on to change the face of warfare for ever.

But whether a soldier wielded a saber, struggled with an obsolete smoothbore musket, carried a multi-shot revolver, poured rapid fire from a magazine repeating rifle or took his place in the crew of a cannon – in the end it was the spirit, courage and determination of the fighting man that really counted. To face up to a storm of bullets, shot and shrapnel without flinching, taking cover or running away takes a special form of courage. One which was displayed repeatedly by all kinds of men, no matter the cause they fought for or the weapons they used. Remember this and wonder as you peruse this book.

An unknown infantry company equipped with Model 1842
Muskets after decorating their camp with a spectacular archway.

CHAPTER ONE

Pistols and Revolvers

Even before the war, the handgun was seen as an essential personal defense tool for the traveler, householder, settler and cowhand, especially in the more lawless regions of the West. So when men flocked to join up, many brought their own pistols and revolvers, whether to be used as their main weapon or as a handy backup in a crisis. The rapidly expanding armies themselves struggled to provide anything like enough weapons, so pressed into service pretty much anything they could get their hands on. Enterprising business men on both sides set up large and small factories to fill the gaps, sometimes by simply copying the best designs available. Overseas manufacturers were also quick to spot the opportunity, and many guns flowed in from Britain and Europe.

So, while the popular image may be of men equipped solely with fine Colts or Remingtons, in reality, both sides had a widely varied array of sidearms. Some unfortunate soldiers went to war with single shot muzzleloaders, such as the government pattern Model 1842, or percussion conversions from the earlier flintlock Model 1836. However, the majority were equipped with some form of percussion revolver, while some had cartridge revolvers, and a few even had early repeating magazine pistols.

The revolver had first come into widespread use in the middle of the nineteenth century. Other designers had created earlier revolver-like devices, but it wasn't until Samuel Colt combined the different elements of revolving cylinder, single barrel, indexing mechanism and percussion ignition in a reliable, effective package that the revolver became a practical possibility. Colt developed his idea and patented it in 1836, but it took some years before his ideas received anything like general acceptance.

His patent expired in 1856, allowing others to manufacture directly competing weapons, but it took the outbreak of war to really put the revolver on the map. Manufacturers sprung up on both sides, some with their own designs and some with straightforward Colt copies.

At this time most revolvers made in America were single-action, in that the user had to manually cock the weapon first, usually by thumbing back the hammer, which also positioned the cylinder. All the firer then had to do was aim and pull the trigger to fire. It made for a relatively slow rate of fire, but it did mean that careful aimed shots were easier. Single-action mechanisms are also simple, with very little to break or go wrong – a popular feature for users who could be hundreds of miles away from the nearest armorer.

Self-cocking revolvers were more popular in Britain and Europe, where the user simply had to apply a single pull on the trigger to cock then fire the weapon. The ability to fire quick snapshots was seen as useful in a close-range brawl, although the downside was that accurate long-range fire was less easy. Eventually the double-action lock was

*The Confederacy always had problems in finding sufficient modern weapons for their
soldiers, as demonstrated by the obsolete single-shot percussion muzzleloader carried
by Private Robert Patterson of Co. D, 12th Tennessee Infantry.*

A Confederate soldier with a fine array of armaments. A pair of Colt Navy .36 caliber pistols are tucked in his belt, while he carries a Model 1855 single-shot percussion muzzleloader. When fitted with the shoulder stock (as seen here) the Model 1855 was intended to be a short carbine, but was not a great success. Too light to be an effective carbine, but too large for a pistol, it was soon superseded by more effective replacements

invented, giving the option of both methods of fire. The best-known design was that by Robert Adams and Lt Beaumont in Britain, and both this revolver and many other British imports were used widely in the war.

Revolvers firing metal cartridges were just beginning to find acceptance as the war started, and by a mixture of clever business deals, effective products and lucky timing this market was dominated by the designs of Smith and Wesson. As with the original Colt revolvers, designers attempted to circumvent Smith and Wesson's patents with varying degrees of success.

What were all these handguns used for? Only effective at very close range and after constant practise, they were completely overshadowed in a large-scale battle by their longarm brethren. Two main groups of soldiers found them useful though. Officers needed to be highly visible in battle, usually using their sword to draw attention to themselves and to signal orders to their men. They needed their hands unencumbered, and a handgun was an ideal compromise of firepower and portability. In this case the sidearm was also seen as a badge of rank, helping to differentiate between commanders and their men.

Revolvers were also extensively used by men on horseback. In this case they needed a weapon that could be aimed and fired with one hand, and one that didn't need to be reloaded in the saddle after every shot.

But many more soldiers than these used handguns, and it was not uncommon to see a rifle-equipped infantryman with a pistol of some kind stuffed into his waistband in case of emergency. In practice these were rarely used, but they did provide a degree of comfort as Billy Yank and Johnny Reb marched off to war.

Fancy copper powder flask with American eagle of the type carried by many Union soldiers in the early days of the war. Loose powder was quickly replaced by pre-filled cartridges of paper, fabric or metal.

Allen & Wheelock 2nd Type Sidehammer Revolver

During the period of the Civil War, the gunsmith Ethan Allen (no relation to the revolutionary hero) traded from Worcester, Massachusetts as "Allen and Wheelock." The company is best known for a series of simple revolvers. Shown here are two of Allen's lighter, small caliber revolvers, each with the barrel screwed into the frame, a spur trigger and a hammer mounted on the right-hand side.

Small caliber revolvers were often privately purchased as a secondary weapon by both officers and soldiers. The example above is chambered for the .32 cartridge, and has a 5-inch barrel inscribed on its left flat with the name "C. Mingay 11th Mass. Battery"

This one is in .22 caliber with a 3-inch octagonal barrel and is fitted with ivory grips.

SPECIFICATIONS

Type: : five-round, single-action, revolver

Origin: Allen & Wheelock, Worcester, Massachusetts

Caliber: .22 and .32

Barrel Length: 3 in and 5 in

Allen & Wheelock Center Hammer Army Revolver

This large revolver was chambered for the .44 cartridge and the smooth-sided cylinder housed six rounds. It had a 7.5-inch barrel, the rear half octagonal, the forward half round, and walnut grips. It was finished in blue, with case-hardened hammer and trigger guard. Only about 700 were manufactured in 1861–2 making this weapon, serial numbered 22, very rare.

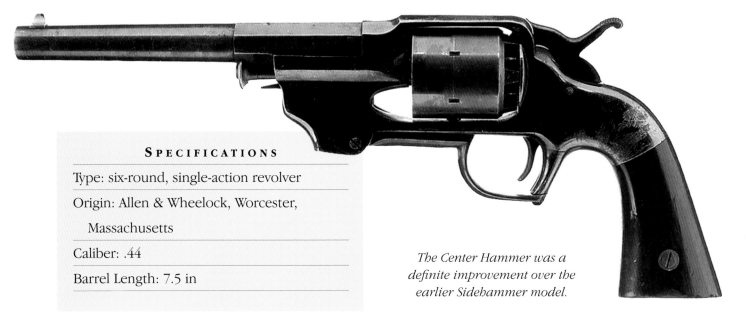

SPECIFICATIONS

Type: six-round, single-action revolver

Origin: Allen & Wheelock, Worcester,
    Massachusetts

Caliber: .44

Barrel Length: 7.5 in

The Center Hammer was a definite improvement over the earlier Sidehammer model.

Ames Model 1842 Navy Pistol

SPECIFICATIONS

Type: service percussion pistol

Origin: N.P. Ames, Springfield, Massachusetts

Caliber: .54

Barrel Length: 6 in

The single-shot muzzleloading percussion pistol may have been obsolete by the time of the war, but in the scramble to equip the hurriedly-formed armies many were pressed into service. The Model 1842 series had been the first major government issue percussion pistol to be made as such from new, rather than from converted flintlock weapons. With a heavier stock and butt than its army counterpart, the Model 1842 Navy had a brass barrel band and butt cap, while the hammer pivot and spring are actually on the inside of the lockplate. As was typical of the time, contracts for manufacture were let to a number of independent businesses. N.P. Ames were better known for their swords and edged weapon than for firearms, but they did get a contract to produce some 2,000 of this pistol.

A handsome gun but clearly one from a bygone era.

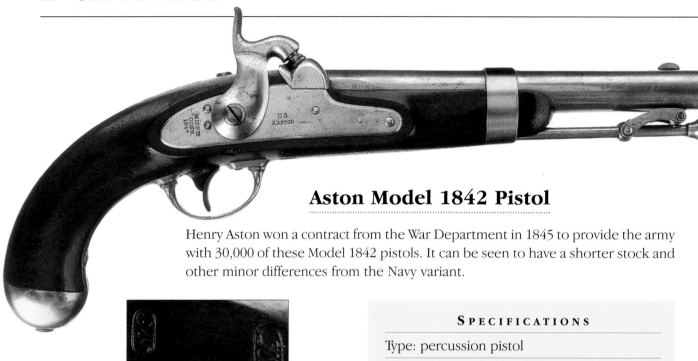

Aston Model 1842 Pistol

Henry Aston won a contract from the War Department in 1845 to provide the army with 30,000 of these Model 1842 pistols. It can be seen to have a shorter stock and other minor differences from the Navy variant.

Inspectors' cartouches as crisp as the day they were stamped.

SPECIFICATIONS

Type: percussion pistol

Origin: H. Aston & Co, Middleton,

    Connecticut

Caliber: .56

Barrel Length: 8.5 in

Another Aston Model 1842 with minor differences in butt cap and lock. The inset clearly shows the Aston trademark on the lockplate.

Beaumont-Adams Percussion Revolver

This revolver is typical of the many thousands of foreign weapons that were procured by both sides in the war, both privately and by the respective governments. Overseas weapons came from a range of sources, with the arms manufacturers of England providing the majority.

The Beaumont-Adams shown here is also significant in that it was the first successful double-action revolver to be made. Robert Adams was an English gun designer who took out a large number of patents in the middle of the 19th century, while his brother, John was responsible for marketing. Their main business activity seems to have been licensing other companies to produce and market the Adams patents. They achieved some success with a series of self-cocking percussion revolvers which could be fired only by bringing quite heavy pressure on the trigger, which made them relatively inaccurate, except at close range. This problem was overcome in 1855 when a Lieutenant Beaumont of the Royal Engineers invented a double-locking system, which allowed the option of preliminary cocking without affecting the rate of fire. The resulting Beaumont-Adams revolvers were manufactured in two calibers, the smaller of the two, in .44, being seen here.

SPECIFICATIONS

Type: six-round, percussion revolver

Origin: Adams Patent Small-Arms Co.,
   London, England

Caliber: .44

Barrel Length: 6 in

The boxed example demonstrates how percussion pistols were sold, complete with a full set of tools, a number of balls and a tin of percussion caps, all housed in a handsome box. Even though some of the tools are missing, the box has ensured that this weapon is preserved in excellent condition,

This unboxed Beaumont-Adams is somewhat battered and has clearly seen some active service – but that, of course, was precisely what it was designed to do.

Brooklyn Firearms Pocket Revolver

The war took place at a time when metallic cartridges were becoming an acceptable replacement for percussion-fired ball and powder ammunition. But as Rollin White held the patent on drilled-through revolver cylinders – and sued anyone who tried to infringe it – several inventors sought alternative methods of loading cartridges. One of these was Frank Slocum, whose revolver's cylinder contained five chambers, each covered by a forward-sliding sleeve. To load, the firer placed his fingertip on the serrated section of an exposed sleeve and pushed it forward; he then placed the cartridge in the chamber, closed the sleeve and moved the cylinder through one-fifth of a turn. He then repeated the process until all troughs were full. The Slocum revolver was manufactured by the Brooklyn Fire Arms Co. and some 10,000 were completed between 1863 and 1865.

Slocum's forward-sliding sleeves in the cylinder attempted to bypass the Rollin White patent.

SPECIFICATIONS

Type: five-round, sleeved, revolver

Origin: Brooklyn Fire Arms Co., Brooklyn, New York

Caliber: .32 rimfire

Barrel Length: 3 in

Brooklyn Bridge Colt Copy

Successful weapons were often copied by other manufacturers, either to make a quick profit in peacetime or to create effective weapons as quickly as possible for the fighting armies. Colt's revolvers were probably imitated more than any other manufacturer's, and this one is typical of the many copies that were made of the Colt Pocket series (see later entry). Almost identical to Colt's production, it has a scene of ships under a bridge engraved on the cylinder.

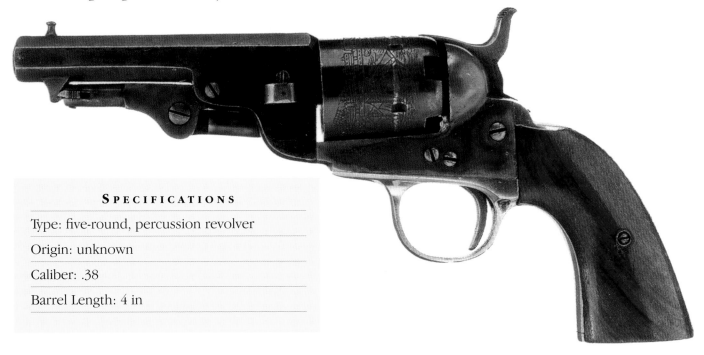

SPECIFICATIONS

Type: five-round, percussion revolver

Origin: unknown

Caliber: .38

Barrel Length: 4 in

Butterfield Army Percussion Revolver

Patented in 1855 by Jesse Butterfield, this design is reminiscent of the earlier "transition" revolvers. It had a unique priming system, where a tubular magazine (accessed from in front of the trigger guard) held paper "pellet-style" percussion primers. When the single-action hammer was cocked, a pellet was slid over the cylinder nipple at the firing position. The Butterfield was ordered in small numbers by the US government, but the contract was canceled after only about 600 were delivered. A few saw service on both sides during the war.

SPECIFICATIONS

Type: 5-shot, single-action percussion revolver

Origin: Jesse Butterfield, Philadelphia,
    Pennsylvania

Caliber: .41

Barrel Length: 7 in

The Butterfield had a distinctive, if not clumsy, appearance.

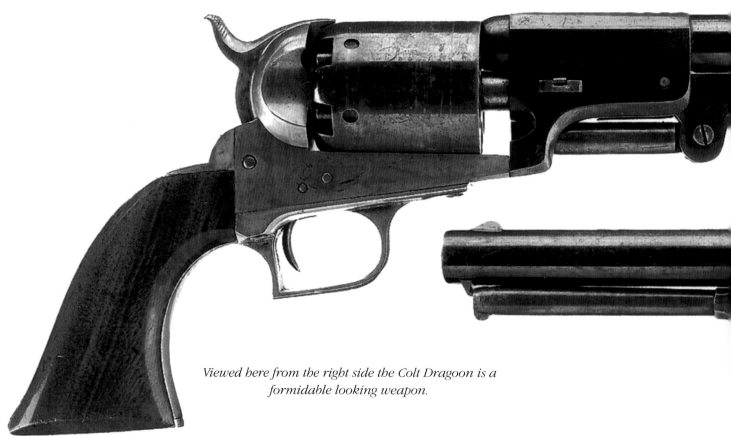

Viewed here from the right side the Colt Dragoon is a formidable looking weapon.

Colt Dragoon 1st Model

The earlier Colt Walker revolver (also known as the Whitneyville-Walker or Colt Model 1847) was designed for use by the Army's U.S. Mounted Rifles (USMR), which were also known by their European name of "Dragoons." The Walker was a six-shot, .44 caliber weapon with a 9-inch barrel and an overall length of 15.5 inches, which weighed no less than 4 pounds 9 ounces. This, plus problems of unreliability, led to the development of the Colt Dragoon, or Model 1848, of which some 20,000 were produced for government service between 1848 and 1860, with more made for sale on the civilian market.

All Colt Dragoons carried six .44 caliber rounds in an unfluted cylinder, many of which were engraved with battles scenes and marked "U.S. DRAGOONS." It was a single-action revolver, with a 7.5-inch barrel and an overall length of 14 inches; weight was brought down to 4 pounds. It was very robust, with the barrel keyed to the chamber axis pin and supported by a solid lug keyed to the lower frame.

The Dragoon was made in three production runs which differed only in minor details, although these differences are of immense importance to today's historians and collectors. The one shown above is the First Model, the main distinguishing mark being that the notches on the cylinder are oval-shaped. Some 7,000 First Model Dragoon revolvers were made in 1848–50, and the item shown here was one of those made for individual purchase rather than government contract.

SPECIFICATIONS

Type: single-action percussion revolver

Origin: Colt PFA Mfg Co., Hartford, Connecticut

Caliber: .44

Barrel Length: 7.5 in

The detail shows a clear stamping of Colt's Patent and the U.S. government mark.

The close-up of the frame and cylinder below reveals that the finish on this gun is probably not original.

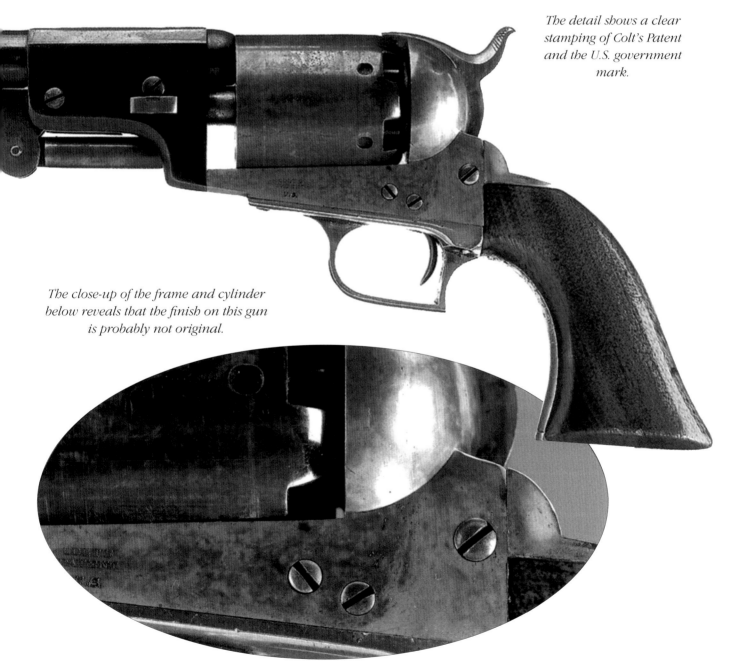

*Colt's .44 caliber models were large pistols, as can be seen
from the pair in the waistband of this Federal cavalryman.*

Colt Dragoon 3rd Model

Building on the success of the Dragoon, Colt introduced a Second Model Dragoon, which differed from the First Model in having rectangular cylinder notches. Some 2,500 were made in 1850 through 1851. The most successful version of the Dragoon, however, was the Third Model, the main production version. Over 10,000 of these were completed in 1851 through 1860, and they can be identified by the round trigger guard, whereas the guards on the earlier two versions were square-backed. The Third Model also had notches for attaching a shoulder stock, although such stocks were seldom, so far as is known, issued. Some late-production Third Model Dragoons (such as the one shown here) had a slightly longer 8 inch barrel.

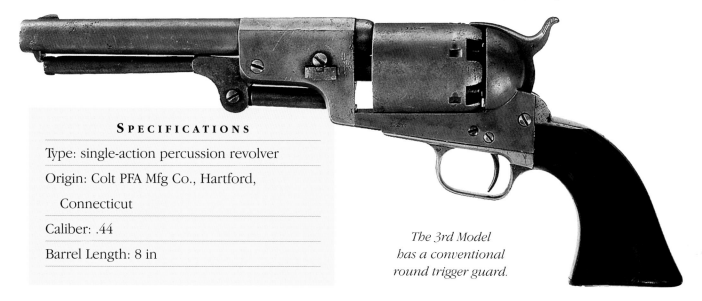

SPECIFICATIONS

Type: single-action percussion revolver

Origin: Colt PFA Mfg Co., Hartford,
    Connecticut

Caliber: .44

Barrel Length: 8 in

The 3rd Model has a conventional round trigger guard.

Colt Model 1848 Baby Dragoon

Even though Samuel Colt was busy producing weapons for the military, he still managed to find the time to design and produce lighter weapons for the civilian market. One of the first of these was the Model 1848, also known as the "Baby Dragoon," a five-round, .31 caliber weapon, of which some 15,500 were produced in 1848 through 1850. These were made with 3-inch, 4-inch, 5-inch or, as seen here, 6-inch barrels. Many saw wartime service as privately purchased secondary weapons.

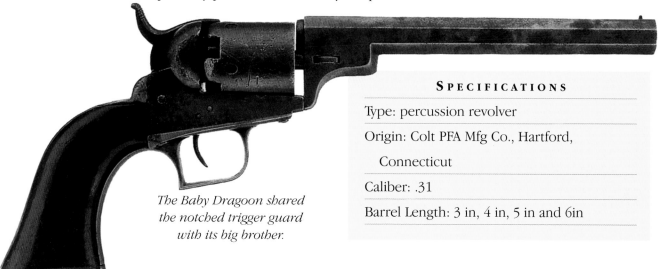

The Baby Dragoon shared the notched trigger guard with its big brother.

SPECIFICATIONS

Type: percussion revolver

Origin: Colt PFA Mfg Co., Hartford,
    Connecticut

Caliber: .31

Barrel Length: 3 in, 4 in, 5 in and 6in

Colt Model 1849 Pocket Revolver

Successor to the Baby Dragoon, the Model 1849 Pocket Revolver was produced in vast numbers, with some 325,000 being completed from 1850 through to 1873. They were made with either 3-inch, 4-inch, 5-inch, or 6-inch barrels and with five-or six-shot cylinders, but there were many more minor variations, as is inevitable over such a long production run.

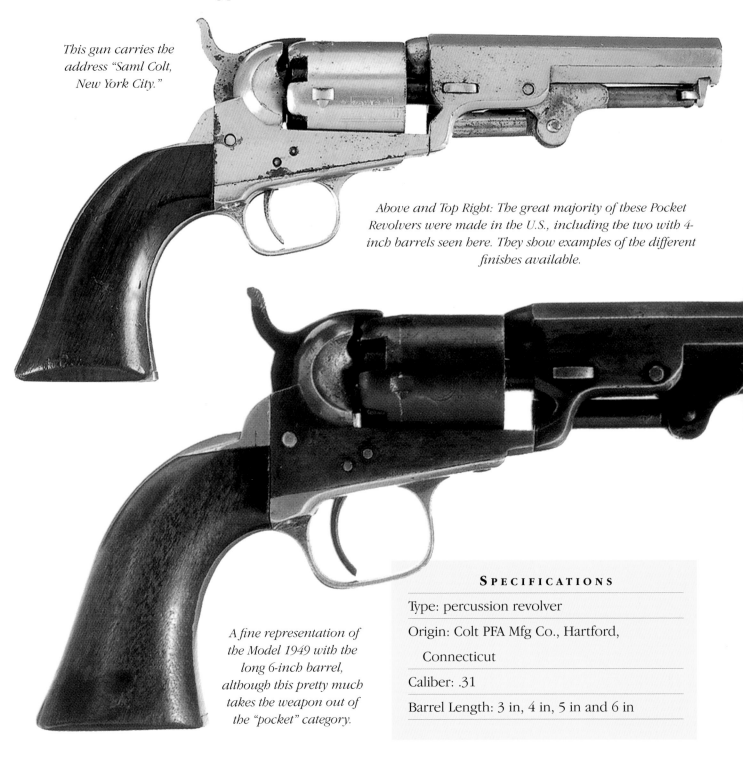

This gun carries the address "Saml Colt, New York City."

Above and Top Right: The great majority of these Pocket Revolvers were made in the U.S., including the two with 4-inch barrels seen here. They show examples of the different finishes available.

A fine representation of the Model 1949 with the long 6-inch barrel, although this pretty much takes the weapon out of the "pocket" category.

SPECIFICATIONS

Type: percussion revolver

Origin: Colt PFA Mfg Co., Hartford, Connecticut

Caliber: .31

Barrel Length: 3 in, 4 in, 5 in and 6 in

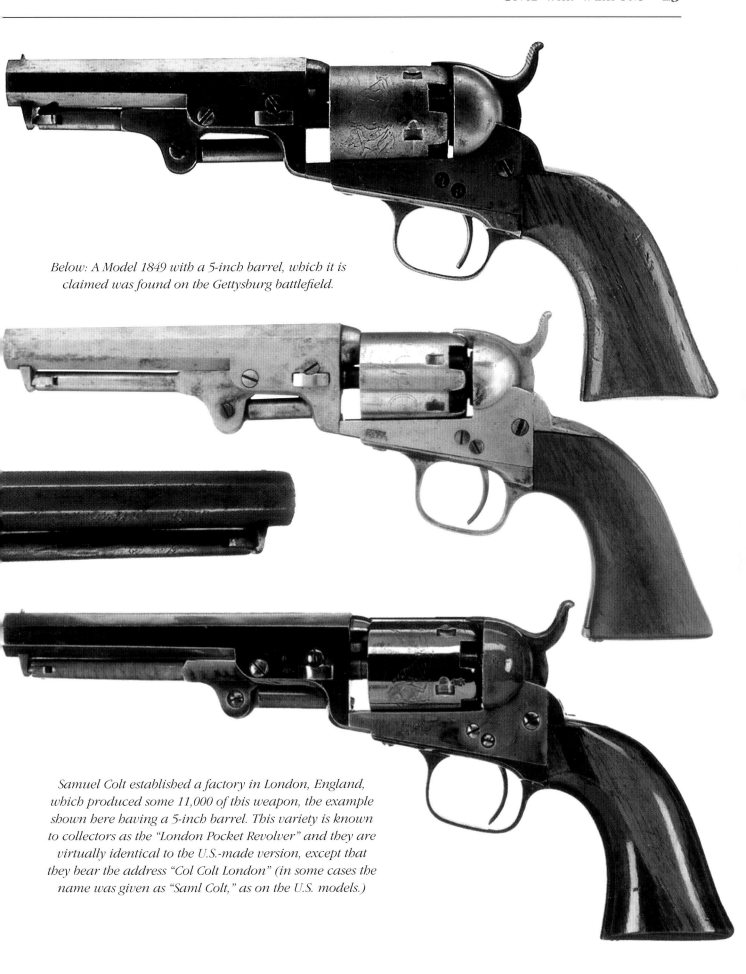

Below: A Model 1849 with a 5-inch barrel, which it is claimed was found on the Gettysburg battlefield.

Samuel Colt established a factory in London, England, which produced some 11,000 of this weapon, the example shown here having a 5-inch barrel. This variety is known to collectors as the "London Pocket Revolver" and they are virtually identical to the U.S.-made version, except that they bear the address "Col Colt London" (in some cases the name was given as "Saml Colt," as on the U.S. models.)

Colt Navy Model 1851

The Colt Model 1851 Navy revolver was one of the most popular handguns ever made, with some 215,000 manufactured in various Colt factories in 1850 through 1873. It has a 7.5-inch octagonal barrel and a smooth sided cylinder which houses six .36 caliber rounds. In most cases, the cylinder was decorated with a scene involving a naval battle between United States and Mexican fleets. It was this decoration that gave the type its "Navy" designation, and the term ended up being used to describe any military percussion revolver in .36 caliber. Revolvers made for .44 rounds were usually called "Army." Many fighting men, whether on land or at sea, preferred the lighter weight and smaller size of the .36, and revolvers of both sizes were used by all branches of the armed forces, whether Federal or Confederate.

A shoulder stock was available for the Model 1851, which could be attached to the butt for more accurate long-range shooting. The company applied three different forms of address on these revolvers, some being marked "Saml. Colt New York City," while others bore "Saml. Colt Hartford, Ct;" and there was a yet further variation of "Saml. Colt New York U.S. America."

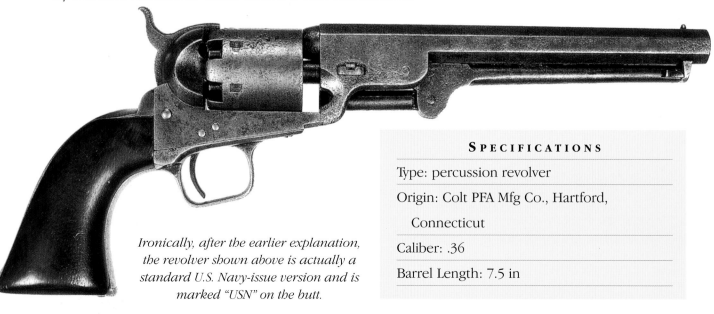

Ironically, after the earlier explanation, the revolver shown above is actually a standard U.S. Navy-issue version and is marked "USN" on the butt.

SPECIFICATIONS

Type: percussion revolver

Origin: Colt PFA Mfg Co., Hartford, Connecticut

Caliber: .36

Barrel Length: 7.5 in

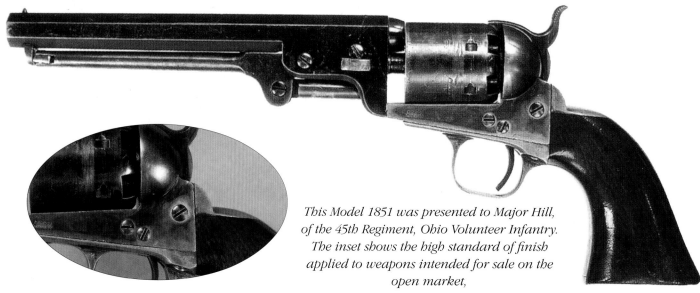

This Model 1851 was presented to Major Hill, of the 45th Regiment, Ohio Volunteer Infantry. The inset shows the high standard of finish applied to weapons intended for sale on the open market,

Major Hill of the 45th Ohio Volunteer Infantry holding his saber and his revolver, posibly the one shown on the left. Note that he has no holster and his gun is simply stuffed into his belt.

Colt Model 1855 Root Revolver

This design was developed by a Colt employee, Elijah Root, and was the company's first-ever, solid-frame design, with a top-strap across the cylinder joining the barrel and frame. It was fitted with a side-mounted hammer, a stud-trigger without guard, and a single-action lock. It was produced in .28 and .31 calibers, but all have a 3.5-inch barrel. It is very popular with modern gun-collectors, who know it simply as "the Root," and who have identified no less than twelve minor variations in the actual production weapons.

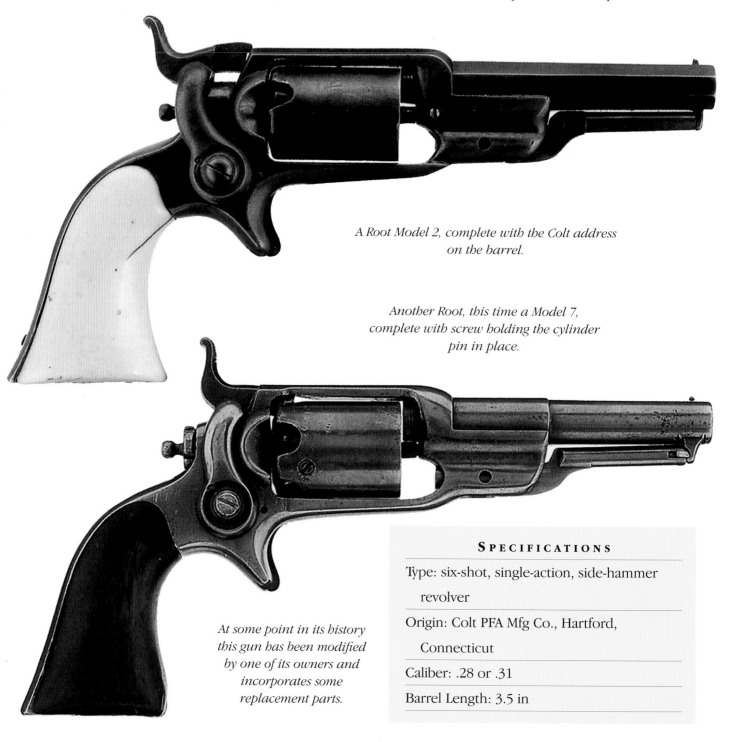

A Root Model 2, complete with the Colt address on the barrel.

Another Root, this time a Model 7, complete with screw holding the cylinder pin in place.

At some point in its history this gun has been modified by one of its owners and incorporates some replacement parts.

SPECIFICATIONS

Type: six-shot, single-action, side-hammer
revolver

Origin: Colt PFA Mfg Co., Hartford,
Connecticut

Caliber: .28 or .31

Barrel Length: 3.5 in

Colt Model 1860 Army

The production figures for the Colt Model 1860 are self-explanatory – the total produced between 1860 and 1873 was 200,500, of which the U.S. government accepted no less than 127,156. Designed as the successor to the Third Model Dragoon (see earlier) it became one of the most widely used of all handguns during the Civil War and was equally popular in both the Union and Confederate armies.

It was a percussion revolver, with rammer loading from the front of the cylinder and any reasonably experienced shooter ensured that he had a stock of paper cartridges close at hand for rapid reloading. The weapon weighed 2.74 pounds and was fitted with either a 7.5-in or 8-in barrel.

SPECIFICATIONS

Type: percussion revolver

Origin: Colt PFA Mfg Co., Hartford, Connecticut

Caliber: .44

Barrel Length: 7.5 in and 8 in

Here is a very early production example, bearing the serial number "360." The weapon has a fluted cylinder and 7.5-in barrel, and, considering its age, is in remarkably good condition. In addition to all that, there is accompanying evidence that the original owner was Mr N. Nickerson of Canton, New York and the provenance is certified in the letter, shown here, from R.L. Wilson, a renowned expert on Colt handguns.

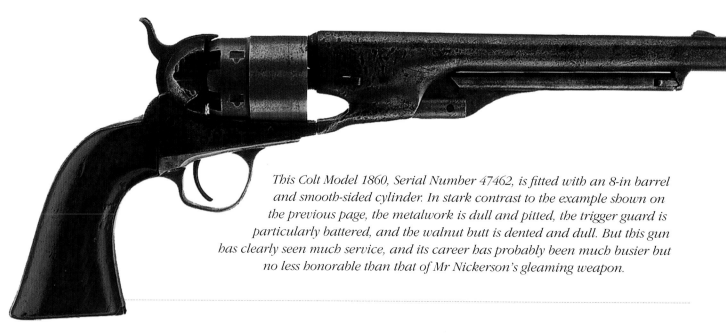

This Colt Model 1860, Serial Number 47462, is fitted with an 8-in barrel and smooth-sided cylinder. In stark contrast to the example shown on the previous page, the metalwork is dull and pitted, the trigger guard is particularly battered, and the walnut butt is dented and dull. But this gun has clearly seen much service, and its career has probably been much busier but no less honorable than that of Mr Nickerson's gleaming weapon.

Colt Model 1861 Navy

Colt also updated the Model 1851 Navy, using a similar smoothly-shaped barrel and rammer shroud to that of the Model 1860 Army. The ensuing design is an elegant and visually appealing weapon with a 7.5-inch barrel and a smooth-sided cylinder housing six shots. Some 39,000 were made, and through its lifetime there were remarkably few variations on the Model 1861.

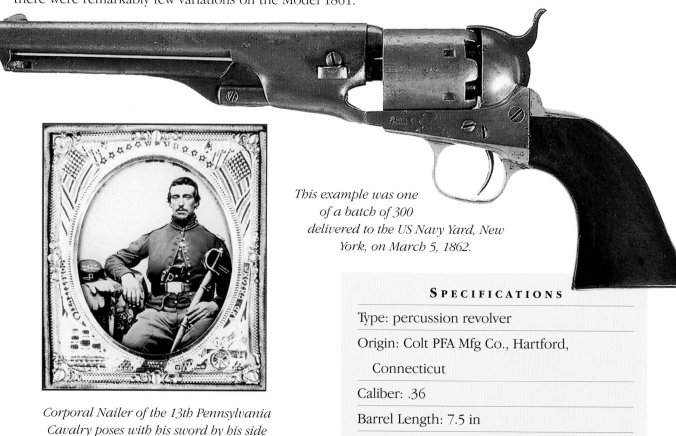

This example was one of a batch of 300 delivered to the US Navy Yard, New York, on March 5, 1862.

Corporal Nailer of the 13th Pennsylvania Cavalry poses with his sword by his side and Colt Navy in his belt.

SPECIFICATIONS

Type: percussion revolver

Origin: Colt PFA Mfg Co., Hartford, Connecticut

Caliber: .36

Barrel Length: 7.5 in

Sergeant Stephen Clinton (right) poses with a comrade from the Sixth Virginia Cavalry. Clinton has a large Colt .44in Army revolver in his belt, while the second man has a smaller Colt, probably a Model 1849.

This Model 1861 is accompanied by what would appear to be its original black leather holster, although it has not stood the test of time so well as the gun.

Colt Model 1862 Pocket Navy

Colt manufactured some 19,000 of these revolvers, which were, in essence, a smaller version of the Model 1851 Navy, chambered for .36 caliber and with a five-shot, smooth-sided cylinder decorated with a roll-on engraving of a Western stage-coach hold-up. The barrels were 4.5, 5.5, or 6.5 inches in length, with the loading-lever attached underneath. The example shown here has a 5.5-inch barrel and is in very good condition.

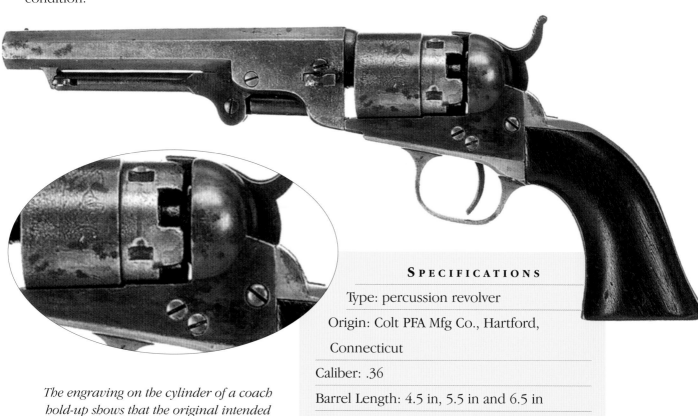

The engraving on the cylinder of a coach hold-up shows that the original intended market was for self protection.

SPECIFICATIONS

Type: percussion revolver

Origin: Colt PFA Mfg Co., Hartford, Connecticut

Caliber: .36

Barrel Length: 4.5 in, 5.5 in and 6.5 in

Cooper Pocket Revolver

James Maslin Cooper was a gunsmith who was in business in Philadelphia from 1850 through 1864 and then at Frankford, Pennsylvania until 1869, when the company ceased to trade. During that time the company's products were limited to a pepperbox and various models of this percussion revolver, based on patents issued to him in 1860 and 1863. There were variants with 4-inch, 5-inch, and 6-inch barrels, but all were chambered for the .31 cartridge. It was unusual for its time in having a double-action mechanism and although some 15,000 were produced the company failed to survive. Illustrated here is an example with a 4-inch barrel and walnut grips.

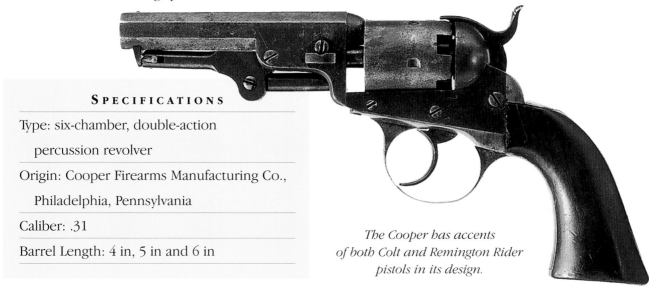

SPECIFICATIONS

Type: six-chamber, double-action
    percussion revolver

Origin: Cooper Firearms Manufacturing Co.,
    Philadelphia, Pennsylvania

Caliber: .31

Barrel Length: 4 in, 5 in and 6 in

*The Cooper has accents
of both Colt and Remington Rider
pistols in its design.*

*Another example of the Model 1842
Navy, this time one of
a batch of 1,200 contracted to
Henry Deringer*

Deringer M1842 Navy Pistol

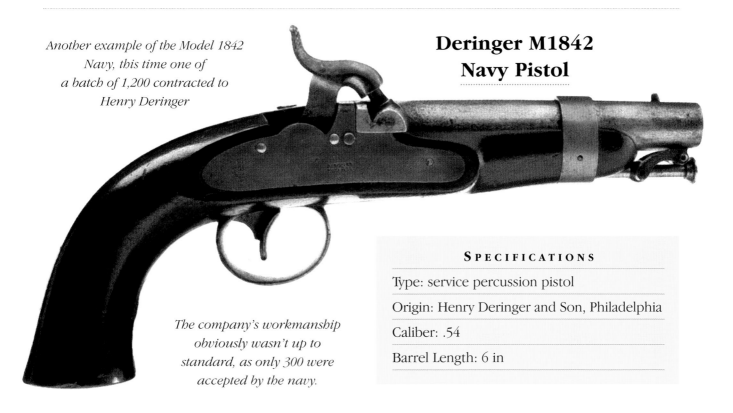

*The company's workmanship
obviously wasn't up to
standard, as only 300 were
accepted by the navy.*

SPECIFICATIONS

Type: service percussion pistol

Origin: Henry Deringer and Son, Philadelphia

Caliber: .54

Barrel Length: 6 in

Deringer Pocket Pistols

Henry Deringer, Senior and his son, Henry Deringer, Junior, were gunsmiths in Philadelphia from the early 1800s until the latter's death in 1869, following which the company struggled on for ten years and then went out of business. The company produced a number of rifle and pistol designs, but by far its most famous product was the large caliber, very small sized, single-shot, caplock, pocket pistol which was widely imitated under the generic name "Derringer" (at some point, and for unknown reasons, the name became misspelled with a double "r"). Deringer pistols were usually produced in matched pairs, although not in the case of the two seen here, one being .45 caliber with a 3.5-inch barrel, while the other is .41 caliber with a 4.3-inch barrel. Not really a military handgun, they were, however, sometimes used as concealable personal defense weapons.

The .45 caliber weapon above would have packed a punch in a tight corner.

An ornate and civilian-looking weapon but one which would still have been pressed into action in the opening days of hostilities.

Eagle Arms Cup-Primer Revolver

Several methods were developed in the 1860s which sought to evade Rollin White's patent and one of these was designed by the Plant Manufacturing Company based in Norwich, Connecticut, which employed a "cup-primer" cartridge. This had a straight-sided, metal case with a dished (cup-shaped) base and was pushed into the chamber from the front. The base of the cartridge was struck by the nose of the hammer through a small hole in the rear-face of the chamber. The Plant revolver was made in .41 and .36 caliber, but the Eagle Arms Company produced the smaller version, seen here in .31 caliber (Eagle Arms was another brand-name used by the Johnson & Bye company). This revolver had a 3.5-inch barrel, smooth-sided cylinder and spur trigger. The slot which can be seen behind the cylinder houses the ejector-rod which was pushed forward through the hammer-aperture in rear of each cylinder to eject the empty cartridge case forward.

The frame of the Eagle Arms revolver was a single brass casting.

SPECIFICATIONS

Type: five-round, double-action, cup-primer
revolver

Origin: Johnson, Bye & Company, Worcester,
Massachusetts

Caliber: .31

Barrel Length: 3.5 in

Hammond Bulldog Pistol

A single shot self-defense weapon in the deringer class, this crudely finished breechloading pistol fired a powerful .44 cartridge and was patented in 1864. It would be effective enough at close range, and pistols of this nature became popular with many soldiers in the Civil War, who bought them to carry as concealed last-ditch back-up weapons.

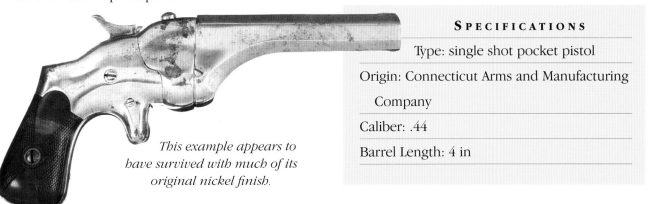

This example appears to have survived with much of its original nickel finish.

SPECIFICATIONS

Type: single shot pocket pistol

Origin: Connecticut Arms and Manufacturing
Company

Caliber: .44

Barrel Length: 4 in

Lindsay 2-shot Pistol

While Colt's patent held, other manufacturers tried all kinds of methods to get multiple shots from a handgun. One of the more unusual attempts was this muzzleloading percussion pistol, designed in 1860 by John P. Lindsay. It had two charges and projectiles, one behind the other, in the same barrel, and the twin hammers were designed to fire them sequence. The Lindsay mechanism was also tried on a musket, but in no case was it successfully adopted. Only 100 of this pistol were made.

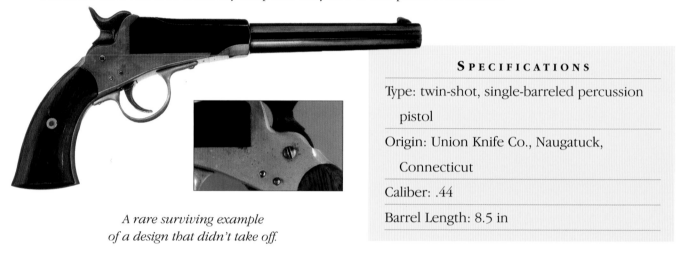

*A rare surviving example
of a design that didn't take off.*

SPECIFICATIONS

Type: twin-shot, single-barreled percussion
    pistol

Origin: Union Knife Co., Naugatuck,
    Connecticut

Caliber: .44

Barrel Length: 8.5 in

Hollis & Sheath Model 1851 Adams Dragoon

Hollis and Sheath were one of the many British gunsmiths who manufactured Adams patent revolvers. The percussion weapon shown here is built to Adams' Model 1851 design, and is self-cocking only (as can be seen by the lack of spur on the hammer). While Adams self-cocking revolvers were less accurate than single-action types such as the Colts, their rate of fire made them useful for self-defense in a fast-moving close-quarters fight. The Adams designs also had integral top straps which made them generally more robust than open-frame types.

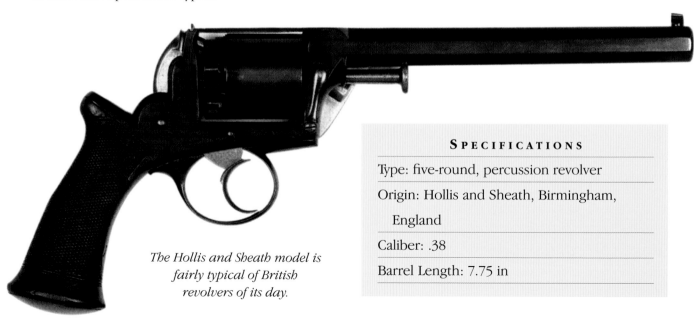

*The Hollis and Sheath model is
fairly typical of British
revolvers of its day.*

SPECIFICATIONS

Type: five-round, percussion revolver

Origin: Hollis and Sheath, Birmingham,
    England

Caliber: .38

Barrel Length: 7.75 in

Lefaucheux Pocket Revolver

The pinfire cartridge was invented by a Frenchman, Casimir Lefaucheux, in 1828 and was in fairly wide use in Continental Europe by about 1840. At the time many felt that centerfire designs, with the primer on the bottom of the cartridge case, weakened the case and risked it bursting to the rear when fired. Pinfire cartridges had their primer embedded within the cartridge, and a metal pin sticking sideways out of the case. As can be seen from this model, the hammer comes down on the edge of the cylinder, striking the pin and driving it into the cartridge, igniting the primer.

Casimir's son, Eugene, designed a series of revolvers which made use of the pinfire principle and was soon producing his designs for many European armies and navies; many were also exported to the United States and used by both sides during the Civil War. The one shown here is in 12 mm military caliber example. Plain and unadorned, with a 6.1-in barrel it is a functional and effective weapon. Notice the recurved tang under the trigger guard which allows the second finger to wrap around the guard. The pinfire system didn't last long, as the cartridges themselves were relatively fragile, they had to be loaded into the cylinder at exactly the correct angle, while centerfire cartridges proved themselves to reliable, effective and easier to use.

Although this French revolver has almost a toy-like appearance, the 12 mm cartridge would have given it an unexpected punch.

Intricate engraving on the frame and cylinder shows the care that went into manufacture.

SPECIFICATIONS

Type: pinfire pocket revolver

Origin: F. Lefaucheux, Paris, France

Caliber: 12 mm pinfire

Barrel Length: 6.1 in

Manhattan Navy

The Manhattan firearms company were one of the many who began manufacturing revolvers when Colt's patent expired. Their main products were copies of the Model 1851 Navy and Model 1949 pocket series, and were so close that Colt took legal action to have production stopped. Even so, over 80,000 Manhattan revolvers were made.

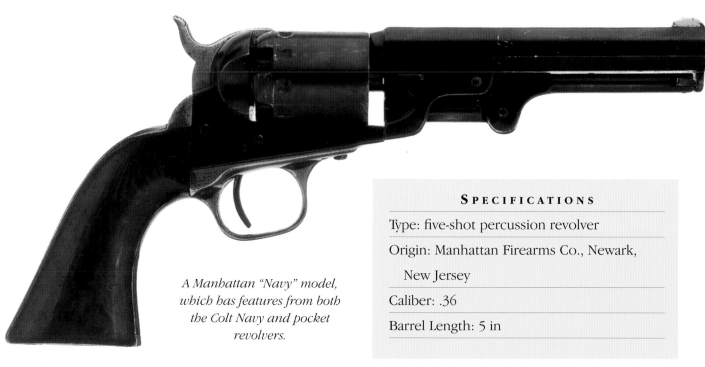

A Manhattan "Navy" model, which has features from both the Colt Navy and pocket revolvers.

SPECIFICATIONS	
Type: five-shot percussion revolver	
Origin: Manhattan Firearms Co., Newark, New Jersey	
Caliber: .36	
Barrel Length: 5 in	

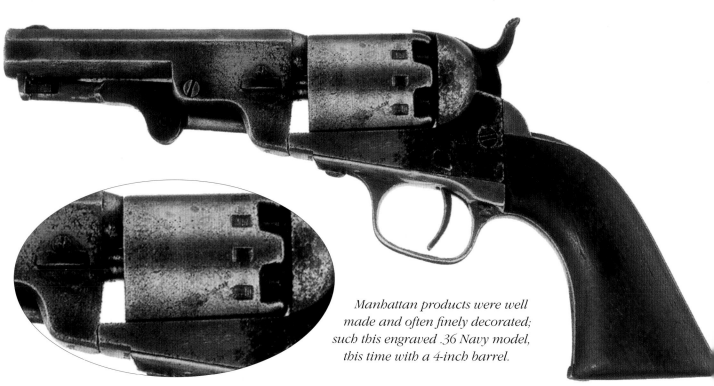

Manhattan products were well made and often finely decorated; such this engraved .36 Navy model, this time with a 4-inch barrel.

Manhattan Tip-up

Another Manhattan product, this time closely resembling the Smith and Wesson cartridge revolver. Firing a .22 rimfire cartridge, it has fine engraving on both the barrel and cylinder. This is the Second Model; the First had more rounded edges to the frame and fired a shorter cartridge (and so had a shorter cylinder). They were popular and well-made weapons such that over 17,000 were made before a lawsuit stopped production.

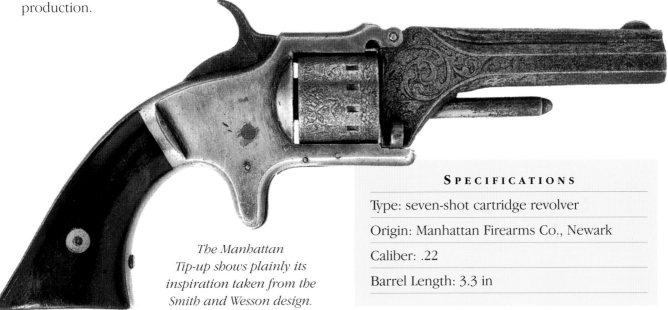

The Manhattan Tip-up shows plainly its inspiration taken from the Smith and Wesson design.

SPECIFICATIONS

Type: seven-shot cartridge revolver

Origin: Manhattan Firearms Co., Newark

Caliber: .22

Barrel Length: 3.3 in

Massachusetts Arms Co. Dragoon Percussion Revolver

The Massachusetts Army Company operated at Chicopee Falls, Massachusetts from 1849 to 1876, during which time it produced rifles and revolvers under licence from other patent-holders. One such was Daniel Leavitt of Cabotsville whose design was produced first by Wesson, Stevens & Miller at Hartford, and subsequently by the Massachusetts Arms Co., and is now commonly known as the "Wesson and Leavitt." This example, made in the early 1850s shows the good finish and neat design.

The gun is solidly engineered with a forged sidehammer and underslung cylinder.

SPECIFICATIONS

Type: percussion revolver

Origin: Massachusetts Arms Company, Chicopee Falls, Massachusetts

Caliber: .40

Barrel Length: 7.1 in

Massachusetts Arms Co. Maynard Primed Revolver

This weapon was made by the Massachusetts Arms Company and incorporated, under license, a number of elements whose patents were owned by other people. Dr Edward Maynard of Washington DC was both a dentist and a prolific inventor, and he became aware that others had designed strip-primer systems, but that they all failed because the primer (chlorate of potash) was in a continuous strip and often suffered from burn-through; i.e., a slow but continuous burning rather like a slow-match. Maynard's patented solution to this problem was a new type of tape in which the primer was laid in small pellets at regular intervals between two narrow strips of paper. Thus, provided the mechanism of the firearm was properly designed to feed the tape so that the hammer always hit a pellet, there was no longer any problem of burn-through. Maynard set up the Maynard Gun Company at Chicopee Falls and licensed his patent to other gun makers, such as the nearby Massachusetts Arms Company.

The picture shows the revolver in its case, complete with tools and powder flask. There is a roll of primers in the box immediately behind the butt, still wrapped in its original greaseproof paper.

This beautifully preserved example in its original case with tools, powder flask, and priming caps, makes it a very desirable purchase for any collector.

SPECIFICATIONS

Type: Maynard tape-primed revolver

Origin: Massachusetts Arms Company, Chicopee Falls, Massachusetts

Caliber: .28

Barrel Length: 2.5 in

Metropolitan Navy Percussion

When the Colt factory was damaged by fire in 1864, the Metropolitan Arms Co. began to manufacture copies of Colt weapons. This "Navy" model is almost indistinguishable from the Colt original of the time, even down to the faint remnants of the naval battle scene engraved on the cylinder. It also has a brass trigger guard with walnut grips.

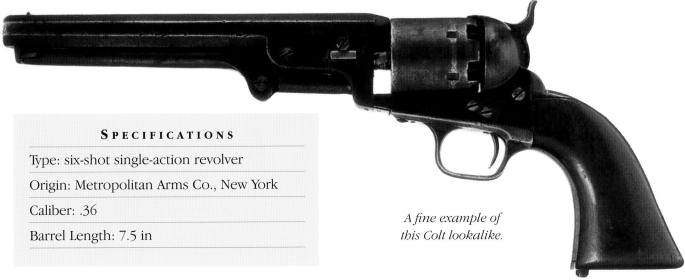

SPECIFICATIONS

Type: six-shot single-action revolver

Origin: Metropolitan Arms Co., New York

Caliber: .36

Barrel Length: 7.5 in

A fine example of this Colt lookalike.

National No. 2 Deringer

Moore's Patent Firearms Co. was established in Brooklyn in the middle of the 19th century and changed its name to the National Arms Company in 1866. Among its products was the No. 1 Deringer, which was very successful, achieving sales of some 10,000 in 1860–65. This was followed by an improved model which had just entered

SPECIFICATIONS

Type: deringer-type pocket pistol

Origin: National Arms Co., Brooklyn, New York

Caliber: .41

Barrel Length: 2.5 in

production when the name changed and was then marketed as the National No. 2 Deringer (seen here). The No.2 Deringer had a spur trigger and was reloaded by pressing the release catch and swivelling the barrel to expose the chamber. The National Arms Co. was bought by Colt in 1870, following which this weapon continued to be marketed as the Colt No. 2 Deringer.

Nepperhan Revolver

The Nepperhan Fire Arms Company made about 5,000 of these .31 Colt copies during the Civil War.

SPECIFICATIONS

Type: five-shot single-action revolver

Origin: Nepperhan Fire Arms Co., Yonkers, New York

Caliber: .31

Barrel Length: 4.25 in

Palmetto M1842 Pistol

William Glaze and Benjamin Flagg set up the Palmetto Armory, and in 1852–53 made 1,000 of these standard Model 1842 percussion pistols for the South Carolina Militia. Many saw service with Confederate forces during the Civil War, and this one has both 1852 and a C.S.A. stamp on the lock.

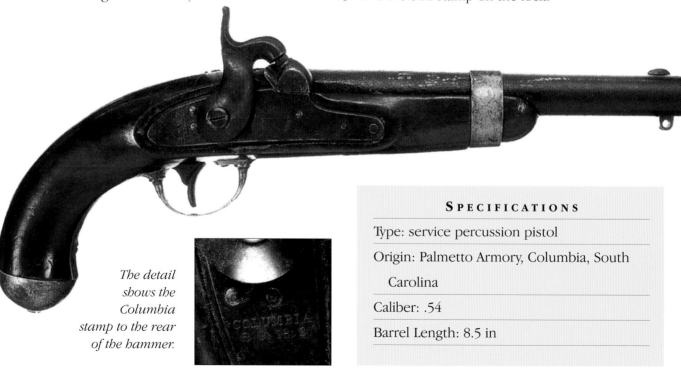

The detail shows the Columbia stamp to the rear of the hammer.

SPECIFICATIONS

Type: service percussion pistol

Origin: Palmetto Armory, Columbia, South Carolina

Caliber: .54

Barrel Length: 8.5 in

Perrin Centerfire Revolver

In 1859, Perrin & Delmas patented the first European centerfire revolver and produced a successful range of weapons. The large European-style centre-fire revolver shown here was one of the many foreign weapons that found their way into the hands of American fighting men during the Civil War. Some 550 or so were purchased by the Federal Government and others were bought privately. A heavy and powerful enough weapon, it must have been difficult for an American owner to find a reliable supply of the 11 mm centerfire cartridges it used.

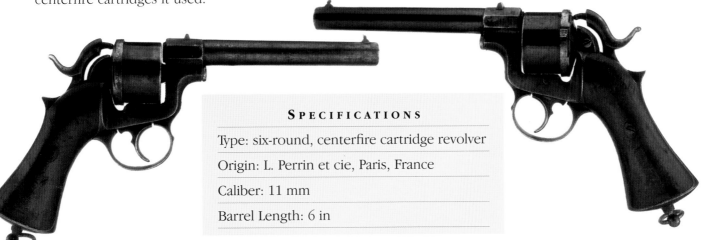

SPECIFICATIONS

Type: six-round, centerfire cartridge revolver

Origin: L. Perrin et cie, Paris, France

Caliber: 11 mm

Barrel Length: 6 in

Pettengill Army Model

Although this revolver was designed and named after Charles Pettengill, it was actually manu-factured by Rogers, Spencer and Co. Pettengill designed the self-cocking firing mechanism, with the hammer completely enclosed within the frame. The firer just pulled the trigger to index the cartridge, raise then drop the hammer. There was no provision for single-action fire, and the heavy

SPECIFICATIONS

Type: six-shot self-cocking revolver

Origin: Rogers, Spencer & Co., Willow Dale, New York

Caliber: .44

Barrel Length: 6.5 in

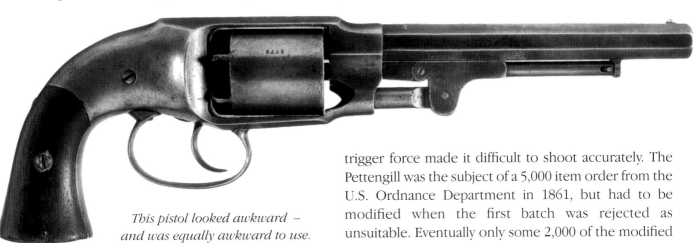

This pistol looked awkward – and was equally awkward to use.

trigger force made it difficult to shoot accurately. The Pettengill was the subject of a 5,000 item order from the U.S. Ordnance Department in 1861, but had to be modified when the first batch was rejected as unsuitable. Eventually only some 2,000 of the modified weapon were delivered.

Type: : five-shot single-action revolver

Origin: Remington Armory, Ilion, New York

Caliber: .31

Barrel Length: 3 in

Remington-Beals 1st Model Pocket Revolver

One of the reasons for the success of the Remington Armory was the company's willingness to take the best designs from wherever they could find them. As a result, the Armory had become a magnet for many skilled engineers and designers, and one such was Fordyce Beal. After an earlier stint at Remington, he went to the Whitneyville Armory in 1854, but was enticed back to Remington after only two years. Back at Remington, he helped the company enter the civilian market with its first ever pistol, this first model Remington Beals, patented in June 1856.

A small, reliable and effective single-action 5-shot percussion arm, the basic weapon was subject to significant design changes through its life, and was popular with the serving men of both sides in the war.

Remington-Beals 2nd Model Pocket Revolver

Beal's second model .31 caliber single-action pocket revolver for Remington had some minor improvements over the first. The main difference was that it now had a spur trigger rather than the trigger and guard of the first model. The butt had also been reshaped and squared off, while the grips were now either checkered rubber or, as shown in this case, walnut.

The distinctive spur trigger replaced the more conventional arrangement on the 1st Model.

Remington-Beals 3rd Model Pocket Revolver

Fordyce Beals continued to develop his pocket revolver line with this third model. Larger than the previous two models, it had a 4-inch barrel while keeping the spur trigger and squared butt of the second model. The main distinguishing feature is the solid frame extension under the barrel and the attached pivoting rammer.

SPECIFICATIONS

Type: five-shot single-action revolver

Origin: Remington Armory, Ilion, New York

Caliber: .31

Barrel Length: 4 in

This model has many features that would characterize the company's large frame revolvers.

Remington-Rider Double-Action Revolver

Remington formed another design partnership, this time with Joseph Rider of Newark, Ohio. Rider chose Remington to manufacture his double-action design patented in 1859. It had an unusual "mushroom-style" cylinder with the percussion nipples set in towards the chambers and angled outwards to meet the hammer. The trigger guard was also rather large, with a distinctive straight trigger. Many such weapons were later converted to fire metallic cartridges, and have a claim to be the first American double-action cartridge revolver.

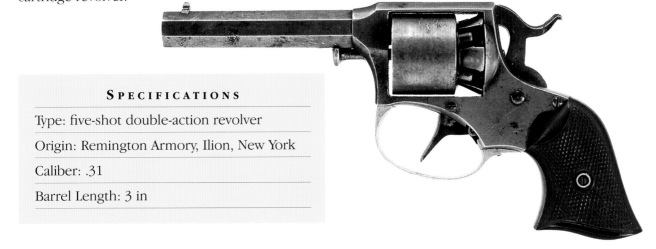

SPECIFICATIONS

Type: five-shot double-action revolver

Origin: Remington Armory, Ilion, New York

Caliber: .31

Barrel Length: 3 in

SPECIFICATIONS

Type: six-shot single-action revolver

Origin: Remington Armory, Ilion, New York

Caliber: .36

Barrel Length: 7 in

A nicely preserved example in original blued finish.

Remington-Beals Navy Revolver

By the end of the 1850s Remington was producing a range of pocket revolvers, pistols and rifles, but had no weapons in the larger "military" calibers. In 1858 Fordyce Beals took the principles of his third model, and developed an entirely new arm in .36 caliber. It had a large solid frame, complete with integral top strap, octagonal barrel and single-action lock. A large hinged ram sat beneath the barrel. This turned out to be a reliable and effective weapon, and was ordered by the US Government as they rearmed in preparation for the Civil War. The first government deliveries to see service were actually the .44 Army version.

SPECIFICATIONS

Type: six-shot single-action revolver

Origin: Remington Armory, Ilion, New York

Caliber: .44

Barrel Length: 8 in

5000 of these guns were ordered at the outset of the war at $15 each by the Federal authorities.

Remington-Beals Army Revolver

When Col. Ripley, the Chief of Ordnance examined the Remington-Beals Navy prototypes, he immediately placed a large order – but for revolvers in .44 Army caliber. This revolver has a similar appearance to the original .36 version but is slightly larger and has a longer barrel. The first deliveries were made in August 1862; the first of a long line of Remington large caliber percussion revolvers.

Remington Model 1861 Army Revolver

Soon after the Remington-Beals military revolvers entered production, the company looked to improve the design. The main difference was a modification to the way the cylinder axle pin was retained. A channel was cut in the top of the rammer arm to allow the pin to be removed easily. The system was patented by Dr Elliott, and the weapon is sometimes referred to as the Model 1861 Elliott's Patent Army Revolver. In service conditions this system was found to be too fragile, and many revolvers had a small screw added to block this channel.

The Model 1861 is also known as the "Old Model Army." It had a distinctive outline, with an integral top strap, large gap in front of the lower edge of the cylinder, and a long sloping web on the loading ram under the barrel. This form set the pattern for all subsequent Remington military percussion revolvers. Solid, reliable and popular, thousands were made and used during the Civil War and after. Many were manufactured at the Remington facility at Utica created to meet the demands of the war, although they bear "Remington, Ilion," markings.

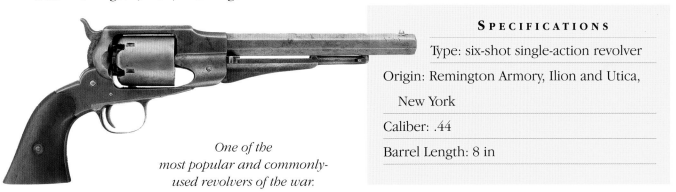

One of the most popular and commonly-used revolvers of the war.

SPECIFICATIONS
Type: six-shot single-action revolver
Origin: Remington Armory, Ilion and Utica, New York
Caliber: .44
Barrel Length: 8 in

Remington Model 1861 Navy Revolver

As with the Remington-Beals designs, a version of the Model 1861 was also produced in .36 caliber. Also referred to as the "Old Model Navy," it followed the same design as its slightly larger brethren. Just as popular as the Army model, thousands also saw hard wartime service.

Its solid frame made the 1861 Model both reliable and accurate.

SPECIFICATIONS
Type: six-shot single-action revolver
Origin: Remington Armory, Ilion and Utica, New York
Caliber: .36
Barrel Length: 7.42 in

Two views of the successful New Model Army. Its great chance came when the Colt factory was largely destroyed by fire, leaving the Remington with little competition for the remainder of the war.

SPECIFICATIONS

Type: six-shot single-action revolver

Origin: Remington Armory, Ilion, New York

Caliber: .44

Barrel Length: 8 in

Remington New Model Army Revolver

Wartime experience showed up some weaknesses in Remington's Model 1861, especially concerning the cylinder fixing system. Remington modified the design by improving the fixing pin and adding safety notches around the rear edge of the cylinder. The end result was one of the finest percussion revolvers ever, and the only one to really challenge Colt's dominance of the military market. Over 120,000 were delivered during the Civil War, and at its peak, production reached over 1,000 a week.

Of course, a version of the New Model was made in .36 Navy caliber, but this didn't sell quite so well – although the 28,000 produced was still a healthy number.

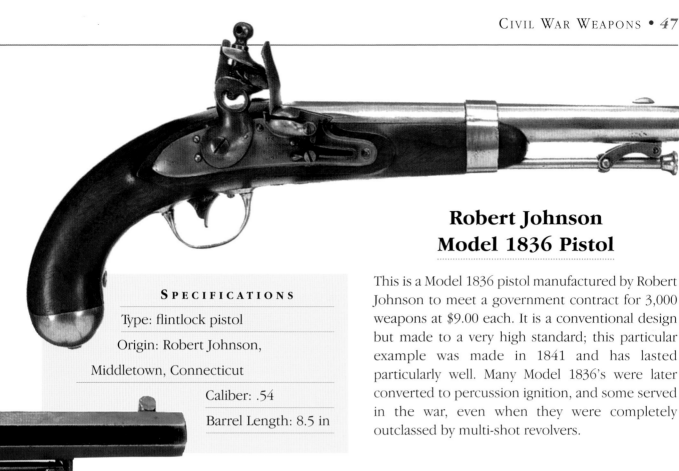

Robert Johnson Model 1836 Pistol

This is a Model 1836 pistol manufactured by Robert Johnson to meet a government contract for 3,000 weapons at $9.00 each. It is a conventional design but made to a very high standard; this particular example was made in 1841 and has lasted particularly well. Many Model 1836's were later converted to percussion ignition, and some served in the war, even when they were completely outclassed by multi-shot revolvers.

Savage Navy Revolver

Edward Savage and Henry S. North started to cooperate in the early 1850s, their only known design being the "Figure-8 Revolver," so named because of the shape of the trigger. These were to a patent held by North and some 400 were produced between 1856 and 1859. Edward Savage then formed the Savage Revolving Firearms Company in 1860 and received two known major government contracts, the first of which was for some 25,000 Model 1861 Springfield muskets. The second contract was for the revolver seen here, which was marked as being to North's patents of 1856, 1859 and 1860, and some 20,000 were produced, of which 11,284 went to the Navy. Our two examples differ in that the one shown here has a smooth cylinder, while the example on the next page has a fluted cylinder.

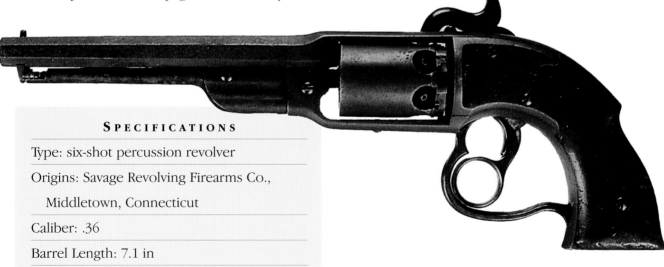

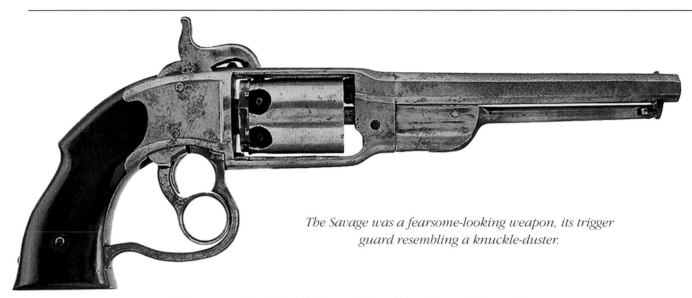

The Savage was a fearsome-looking weapon, its trigger guard resembling a knuckle-duster.

Sharps & Hankins Single-shot Pistol

Christian Sharps (1811–74) was an inventor better known for designing his own rifles, although in the early days he licensed them out to others for production. In 1855, however, he established his own factories in Hartford, Connecticut and Philadelphia, Pennsylvania (the latter becoming Sharps & Hankins in 1863). There, apart from rifles, he also produced designs for one pistol and a number of multi-barrel "pepperpots." His breechloading percussion pistol was produced in various calibers. We show two examples, a .31 pistol with a small frame and a 5-inch barrel, and a .36 pistol with a larger frame and a 6.4-inch barrel.

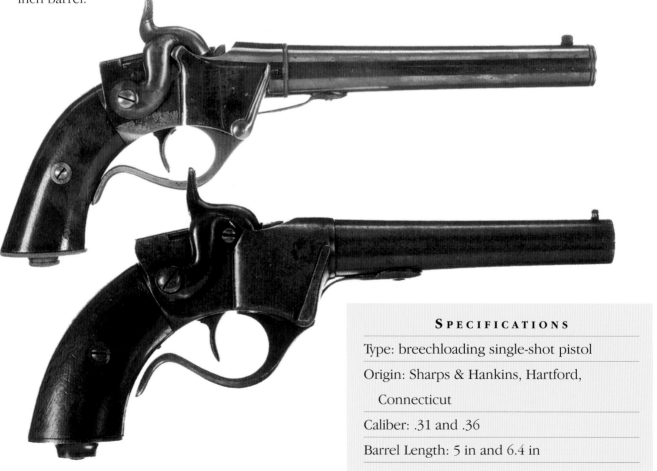

SPECIFICATIONS
Type: breechloading single-shot pistol
Origin: Sharps & Hankins, Hartford, Connecticut
Caliber: .31 and .36
Barrel Length: 5 in and 6.4 in

*Captain Charles Schwartz of the 39th New York demonstrates a formal firing pose
with his Savage .36 revolver. His first finger is on the trigger, while his second
finger holds the unusual cocking lever under the trigger.*

Smith & Wesson Model 2 Army Revolver

After their success with the Volcanic Pistol (see later entry), in 1858 Horace Smith and Daniel Wesson (along with many others) took advantage of the expiry of Colt's master patent and began manufacture of their own revolver design. Smith and Wesson were one step ahead of the others though, in that having purchased Rollin White's patent for a bored-through cylinder, they were able to corner the market for cartridge revolvers.

Their Model 1 was a neat, light personal defense weapon firing a .22 rimfire cartridge. The more powerful Model 2 Army was a straightforward development of the Model 1, and Smith and Wesson had the good fortune that it became available just as the Civil War broke out. Important to this success was that it fired self-contained .32 rimfire cartridges which were not effected by climate or humidity, and it was light enough to be carried as a back-up to rifle or saber. Thus, it was the very latest design and became an immediate success with Union troops, resulting in a huge backlog of orders for the company. The Model 2 had a six-round, fluted cylinder, was chambered for the .32 rimfire round, and was available with 4-, 5-, or 6-inch barrels. Over 77,000 were sold between 1861 and the end of production in 1874.

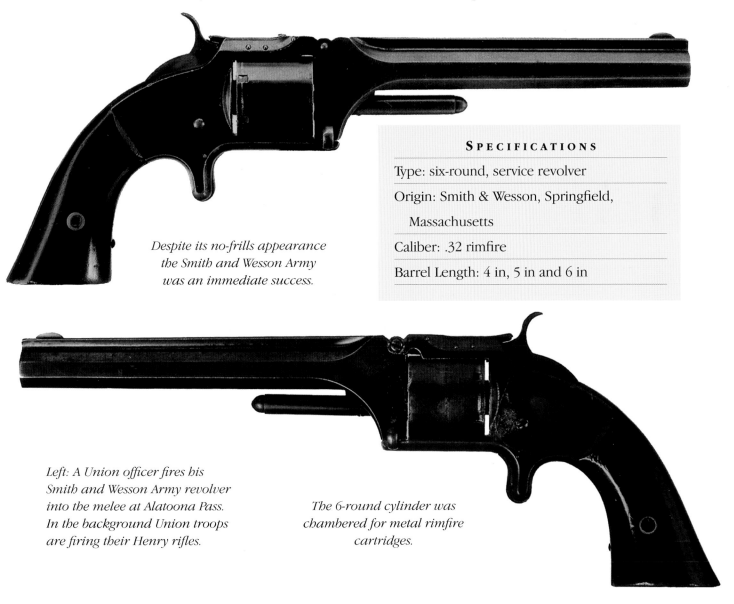

Despite its no-frills appearance the Smith and Wesson Army was an immediate success.

SPECIFICATIONS

Type: six-round, service revolver

Origin: Smith & Wesson, Springfield, Massachusetts

Caliber: .32 rimfire

Barrel Length: 4 in, 5 in and 6 in

Left: A Union officer fires his Smith and Wesson Army revolver into the melee at Alatoona Pass. In the background Union troops are firing their Henry rifles.

The 6-round cylinder was chambered for metal rimfire cartridges.

Spiller & Burr Revolver

On the outbreak of the war, two rich Virginia gentlemen, Edward N. Spiller and David J. Burr, combined with a weapons expert, James H. Burton, to establish a factory to produce a revolver for the Confederate States Army cavalry. The factory was initially sited in Richmond, Virginia, but then moved to Atlanta, Georgia and finally to Macon, also in Georgia, where it set up business in the CSA Armory. The undertaking was always hampered by the pressures of the war, shortage of materials and of skilled labor. The main contract was to deliver 15,000 revolvers in 30 months and had they succeed, Spiller, Burr and Burton would have made a very large profit; in the event, however, only some 1,500 were completed between 1862 and 1865.

Burton's design was based on the Whitney 1858 Navy revolver, and specifically on the Second Model, First Variation, which was in production in the North at the Whitneyville factory, located outside New Haven, Connecticut. Due to shortages of material in the South, however, Burton had to adapt the design in two ways, by using iron instead of steel for the cylinder, and brass instead of iron for the frame.
The example shown here shows both the strong resemblance to the Whitney but has a poorer standard of finish, although there is no reason to think that it did not work as well. Some of the surviving examples are marked with the name "Spiller & Burr" and others with "C.S." (Confederate States.) The story of this revolver highlights the immense industrial disadvantages facing the Confederacy in its struggle against the much better resourced North.

SPECIFICATIONS

Type: six-round, percussion revolver

Origin: Spiller & Burr, Atlanta, Georgia

Caliber: .36

Barrel Length: 7 in

The distinctive brass frame with iron cylinder made for a heavy gun.

Springfield M1855 Pistol Carbine

Designed as a multi purpose arm for cavalrymen, this single-shot pistol was intended to be used as a handgun when mounted and, with the wooden shoulder stock attached, as a carbine when fighting on foot. It came complete with a cavalry-style hinged ramrod, and used the Maynard Tape Priming system. We show two pistols – one with the extension stock and the other without.

Many of these pistols saw service in the early days of the Civil War, although they were soon superseded. Like all such extension arms, they were too large and heavy to be a pistol (and certainly couldn't compete with the revolvers then entering service), but were also too light and short-barreled to make a truly effective carbine.

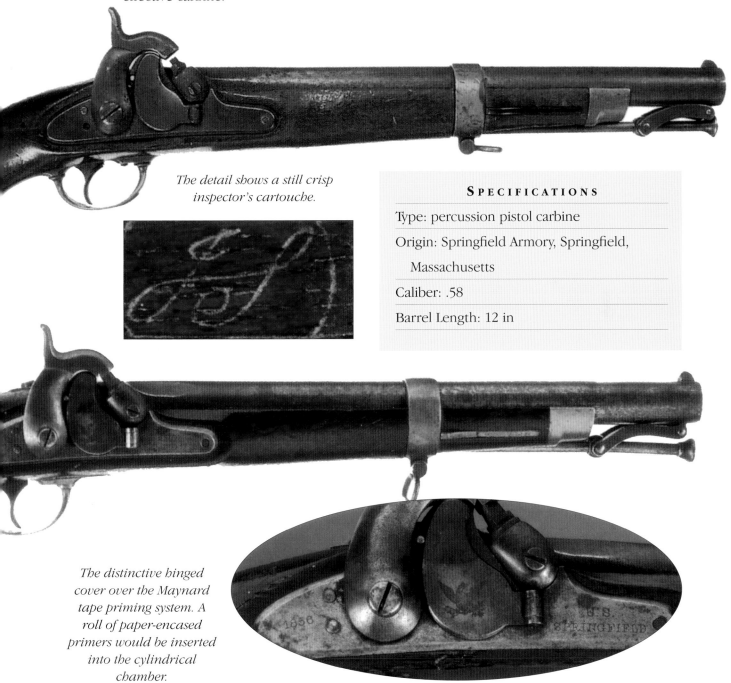

The detail shows a still crisp inspector's cartouche.

SPECIFICATIONS

Type: percussion pistol carbine

Origin: Springfield Armory, Springfield, Massachusetts

Caliber: .58

Barrel Length: 12 in

The distinctive hinged cover over the Maynard tape priming system. A roll of paper-encased primers would be inserted into the cylindrical chamber.

Springfield Arms Revolver

The Springfield Arms Company (which was not related to the U.S. Government's Springfield Armory) was in business from 1851 to 1869, when it was taken over by the Savage Arms Corporation. The general manager, James Warner, patented a number of designs, but he ran foul of Smith & Wesson who sued him for infringing their patents and won, as a result of which Springfield Arms had to hand over some 1,500 weapons.

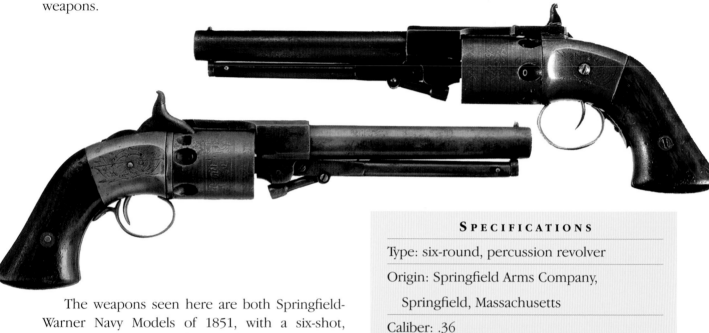

The weapons seen here are both Springfield-Warner Navy Models of 1851, with a six-shot, smooth-sided cylinder, 6-inch .36 caliber barrel and walnut grips.

SPECIFICATIONS
Type: six-round, percussion revolver
Origin: Springfield Arms Company, Springfield, Massachusetts
Caliber: .36
Barrel Length: 6 in

Starr Model 1858 and 1863 Army Revolvers

The Starr Arms Company had its offices on Broadway, New York, and factories at Binghampton, Morrisania and Yonkers. The company manufactured weapons designed by Ebenezer (Eben) T. Starr and also those designed by its president, H.H. Wolcott. The company produced a number of deringers and pepperpots designed by Starr and also a very effective revolver, which appeared in three models: Model 1858 Navy, Model 1858 Army Double-Action and the 1863 Single-Action Army.

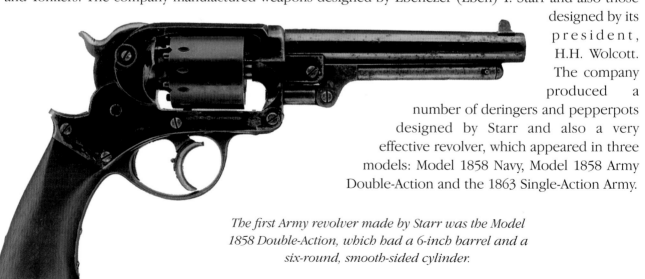

The first Army revolver made by Starr was the Model 1858 Double-Action, which had a 6-inch barrel and a six-round, smooth-sided cylinder.

The Model 1863 was generally similar, but with a single-action and an 8-inch barrel. The company made some 23,000 Model 1858, while some 32,000 Model 1863 were produced between 1863 and 1865.

After the Civil War a number of Model 1863 Single-Action revolvers were converted to rimfire with a new cylinder, breech-plate, and cylinder pin.

SPECIFICATIONS

Type: six-round, single-action, percussion revolver	
Origin: Starr Arms Company, New York, New York	
Caliber: .44	
Barrel Length: 6 in or 8 in	

Starr Model 1858 Navy Revolver

The Starr Model 1858 Navy was a double-action percussion revolver with a 6-inch barrel, similar to the Model 1858 Army but in .36 caliber. Unusually for American revolvers of the time, the mechanism was double action only, such that the hammer could not be cocked by hand to allow a more accurate single-action option. Some 3,000 were made between 1858 and 1860.

SPECIFICATIONS

Type: six-round, double-action, percussion revolver	
Origin: Starr Arms Company, New York, New York	
Caliber: .36	
Barrel Length: 6 in	

The Starr had a slightly European look about it.

Tranter First Model

William Tranter was already a well-established British gunmaker by the time he patented the design of this double action revolver in 1853, two years ahead of Beaumont (see earlier entry). Tranter's method used an unusual double trigger system, where pressure on the lower trigger cocked the hammer. If careful aimed fire was wanted, after the user cocked the hammer with this lower trigger, he would only need light pressure on the upper one to fire. In a close-quarters melee, where rapid (if less accurate) fire was needed, the user just pulled both triggers at once.

Tranter also incorporated a unique safety device, where if the hammer was pulled back a little, a spring-loaded blanking piece inserted itself between the hammer and the percussion nipple. When the hammer was cocked using the bottom trigger, the blanking piece was disengaged.

Early Tranter models were based on Adams (see earlier) frames, as Tranter prefered to pay the fee for a well-proven and solid design than go to the trouble of developing his own.

The one shown here has the Adams frame, and as such is marked "Adams Patent No. 20,580Y."

Tranter's revolvers were made in a range of sizes and calibers, but can be divided into three main classes. The first model, pictured here, usually had a separate detachable ram, although the one shown actually has a non-standard permanently screwed ram. The second model had a larger ram which normally stayed on the weapon, lying along the barrel, but which could be easily removed. The third Model had a permanently mounted ram held on by a screw fitting. Tranters saw extensive service during the war, especially with Confederate forces.

SPECIFICATIONS

Type: five-round, percussion revolver

Origin: William Tranter, Birmingham, England

Caliber: .50

Barrel Length: 8 in

Tranter First Model Pocket Revolver

Tranter revolvers were also made in small pocket sizes, using the same Adams frame and double trigger mechanism of their larger military brethren. Shown here is a First Model with the detachable ram missing. It was one made for a London dealer, and carries their markings: "Wm Powell & Son."

SPECIFICATIONS

Type: five-round, percussion revolver

Origin: William Tranter, Birmingham, England

Caliber: .31

Barrel Length: 3 in

Volcanic Pistols

The Volcanic series of pistols were designed to fire the unusual "Volition Ball," where the bullet formed a self-contained package, complete with propellant and primer in its hollow base. Horace Smith and Daniel Wesson formed their first partnership in 1852 with the aim of producing a repeating pistol where these .41 caliber projectiles were stored in a tubular magazine and chambered using a manually-operated lever, which doubled as the trigger guard. The firer moved this down and forward to extract the used cartridge case and push a new round up and behind the chamber. Pulling the lever backwards then chambered the round and recocked the action.

Speed of firing depended upon how quickly the firer could operate the lever, but it so impressed a journalist from Scientific American that he dubbed the result "volcanic" and the name stuck. The pistol was available with 6-inch, 8-inch, or 16-inch barrels; the example shown here is the 8-inch version, which is clearly marked "SMITH & WESSON, NORWICH. CT." The young company lasted for only two years and then went out of business.

This design clearly incorporates features that would find their way through to the Winchester rifle.

By July 1855, the company had new investors and was trading as the Volcanic Repeating Arms Co., although Smith and Wesson were still involved. All the Volcanics of this period were made for the .41 caliber round, fed from the integral magazine under the barrel. This image shows a "Lever Action Navy Pistol", with a brass frame, 6-inch barrel and flat-bottomed grip and an engraving of an arm holding a dagger.

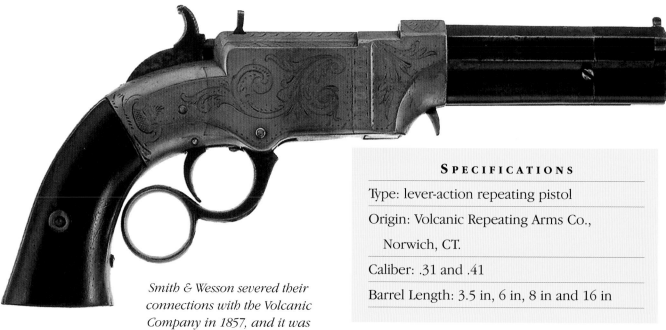

Smith & Wesson severed their connections with the Volcanic Company in 1857, and it was restructured as the New Haven Arms Company. Production of the Volcanic pistols continued, shown by this one clearly marked along the top of the barrel: "New Haven Conn, Patent Feb 14, 1853." The New Haven company used the same frames as the original Volcanics but their pistols were produced in .31 as well as .41 caliber only, with barrels of 3.5 in, and 8 in. There were also some larger pistols and carbine weapons made in this series. The weapon seen here has a brass frame, which is delicately engraved, but silver plate frames were also produced.

SPECIFICATIONS

Type: lever-action repeating pistol

Origin: Volcanic Repeating Arms Co., Norwich, CT.

Caliber: .31 and .41

Barrel Length: 3.5 in, 6 in, 8 in and 16 in

Volcanics were used in small quantities during the Civil War, but were never particularly successful, mainly due to low muzzle velocity and inadequate power. The propellant was also extremely corrosive, causing components to wear out quickly. However, the Volcanic series did introduce tubular magazines, breechloading and lever-operation: all features that were later used to great effect by the Henry rifles and eventually the Winchester repeaters.

Webley Longspur

Philip and James Webley had a gunmaking business in Birmingham from the early nineteenth century, and they eventually became the main manufacturer of service revolvers in the United Kingdom. This early Webley was patented by James in 1853, three years before his death in 1856. Known as the Longspur, it was an open-frame design with the barrel assembly attached to the rest of the frame by the large flat-headed screw visible in front of the cylinder.

There were three models of Longspur – the first model had a detachable ram, the second had a simple swivel ram, and the third the more complex ram shown here. The Longspur is generally known as a single-action revolver, but one shown here is unusual, in that it has a double-action mechanism. Longspurs were used in the war in small numbers.

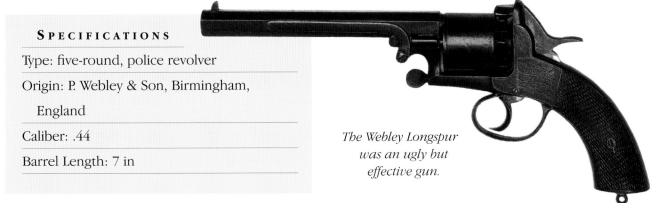

SPECIFICATIONS

Type: five-round, police revolver

Origin: P. Webley & Son, Birmingham,
    England

Caliber: .44

Barrel Length: 7 in

The Webley Longspur was an ugly but effective gun.

Walch Pocket Revolver

Many revolver designers have sought to increase the number of rounds immediately available to the firer by increasing the diameter of the cylinder, but John Walch found a different way – by increasing the length. In this system, the cylinder has five chambers, each of which accommodates two rounds, one behind the other. There are ten nipples and in each cylinder a channel leads from the right nipple to the front load, while the left nipple fires directly into the rear of the chamber. Each separate pull of the trigger fires one round; first the forward round, next the rear round, then to the next cylinder forward round, and so on. These revolvers were manufactured by the New Haven Arms Company (Winchester) at the start of the Civil War.

The elongated cylinder accommodated two rounds end to end in each chamber.

SPECIFICATIONS

Type: ten-round, percussion revolver

Origin: Walch Fire Arms Co., New York, New York

Caliber: .31

Barrel Length: 3.25 in

Warner Pocket Revolver

James Warner (see Springfield earlier) also produced revolvers under his own name, and this neat rimfire cartridge revolver was an attempt in the late 1850s to get back into the pocket revolver business. Although Colt's patent had expired, Warner's cartridge revolvers now ran up against the Rollins White/Smith & Wesson patent, and production was stopped after only 1,000 were made.

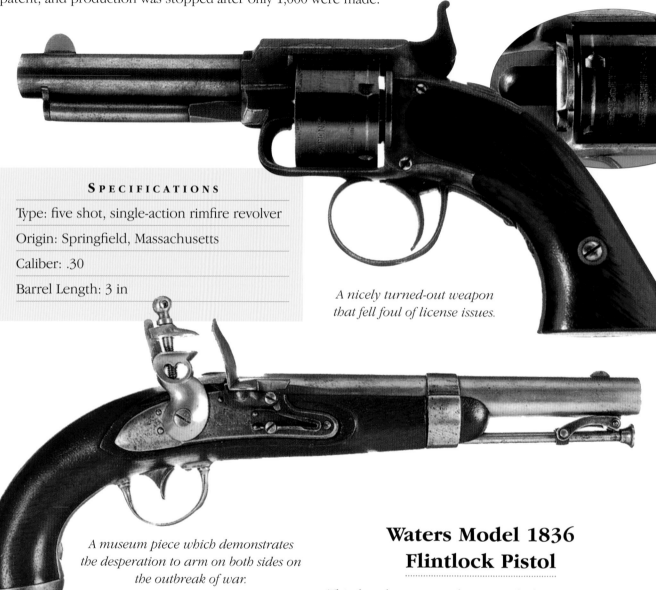

SPECIFICATIONS

Type: five shot, single-action rimfire revolver

Origin: Springfield, Massachusetts

Caliber: .30

Barrel Length: 3 in

A nicely turned-out weapon that fell foul of license issues.

A museum piece which demonstrates the desperation to arm on both sides on the outbreak of war.

SPECIFICATIONS

Type: flintlock pistol

Origin: A. Waters & Co, Millbury, Massachusetts

Caliber: .54

Barrel Length: 8.5 in

Waters Model 1836 Flintlock Pistol

This handsome pistol was made by Asa Waters & Co. at their armory at Millbury, Massachusetts. It was part of a government order placed on September 22, 1836 for 4,000 pistols at US$9.00 each. As is clear from the pictures, this example has been very well maintained over the years and remains in very good condition. Many of these weapons were converted to percussion action, and some were used during the war by those unlucky enough not to be equipped with a revolver.

Waters Flat Lock Pistol

This was one of a batch made by Asa Waters & Co. as a pattern for the Model 1842 percussion pistol, and assembled largely from parts left over from their Model 1836 flintlock pistol contracts. This one has a so-called flat lock and has had the ram pivot installed upside down.

Another version of the popular Model 1842 muzzle-loading pistol.

The Whitney had design similarities to the Remingtons.

Whitney Navy Percussion Revolver

Eli Whitney Sr. was an engineering genius, but perhaps not as effective in business. His invention of the cotton gin revolutionized the economy of the South, but for various reasons, including competition from other manufacturers, Whitney made very little money from it. He then turned his energies to arms manufacture, and from 1798 onwards, Whitney's company produced a range of longarms and revolvers for

both government and civilian markets. Whitney's real strength was in the development of manufacturing techniques, and the company advertised itself as being the first to create standardized parts that could be assembled by workmen with little or no experience.

By the 1860s, the company was in the hands of Whitney's son, Eli Whitney Jr.. Financially it was struggling, and most of its efforts were devoted to assembling and selling weapons from surplus parts bought from the government and from other armories.

The Whitney company's first experience of manufacturing handguns was in 1847 when they made over 1,000 .44 caliber revolvers for Samuel Colt. At that time Colt had no facilities of his own and needed to subcontract the manufacture of a government contract he had been awarded.

Whitney went on to develop weapons to their own design, and by the late 1850s were making this series of military caliber weapons to compete with the Colt Navy types. Unlike the Colts, the Whitney revolvers had a solid frame with integral top strap above the cylinder, making for a stronger and more robust design. The one shown on the previous page is known as the second model, and has an octagonal barrel, brass trigger guard and loading ram under the barrel. The Whitney Navy types proved popular in the Civil War, and over 33,000 were made.

Witton Bros. Tranter Patent Percussion

As did Robert Adams, William Tranter licensed his patents to other manufacturers and retailers who produced their own versions of his double action revolver. This is a later model produced by Witton Brothers, without the Tranter double trigger but with a spurred hammer. It has the Tranter signature lever ram alongside the barrel. This particular item was sold to the Confederate forces during the Civil War, although it never reached them. The shipment was intercepted by Northern Revenue cutter "Harriet Jane" in February 1862.

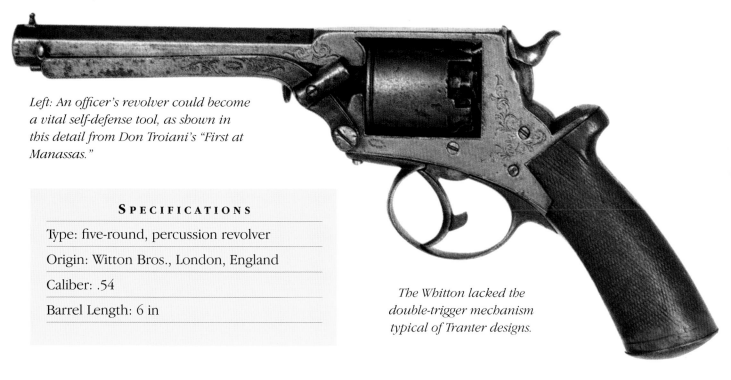

Left: An officer's revolver could become a vital self-defense tool, as shown in this detail from Don Troiani's "First at Manassas."

SPECIFICATIONS

Type: five-round, percussion revolver

Origin: Witton Bros., London, England

Caliber: .54

Barrel Length: 6 in

The Whitton lacked the double-trigger mechanism typical of Tranter designs.

CHAPTER TWO

Cavalry Carbines

Romantic notions of dashing cavalry charges, which attracted young men to enlist on both sides at the beginning of the war, were soon swept away by reality. The traditional purpose of the cavalry to intimidate and scatter infantry, send artillery units into disarray, and generally harry the enemy, which had worked so well in Napoleonic times, was under threat from rapid developments in ballistic weaponry. The techniques of cavalry laid down in the (mainly) French military manuals that both sides had studied belonged to a bygone age.

The useful impact of a cavalry charge against formed-up infantry was seriously in question. A few decades earlier, the foot soldier would only have time for one shot from his inaccurate smooth-bore musket before having to decide whether to face up the onrushing horsemen with cold steel, or to run away.

But with recent improvements in his weaponry, the soldier's effectiveness and killing range were greatly enhanced. Ignition systems such as the percussion cap made longarms much more reliable then before (no more flashes in the pan), while rifled barrels sent a spinning projectile accurately toward the target. Reloading speed was improved and three or more shots could be fired per minute

Spent Minie-type bullet reclaimed from a battlefield site.

with the percussion system as opposed to maybe one with a flintlock action. The projectiles themselves were designed to make the most of rifled barrels. For instance, the Minié bullet was a conical lead slug with a hollow base, the skirt of which expanded when fired to seal the gases in the bore, giving much higher muzzle velocity than the earlier ball, and greatly increased stability in flight. Rifles, in the right hands, were now deadly up to 300 yards. Plenty of time to get a bead on an on-rushing cavalryman.

This situation engendered a new respect for the foot soldier by cavalry. Not one however that was reciprocated. Infantry units would often shout abuse at passing cavalry, and "Whoever saw a dead cavalryman?" was a common taunt. Others more poetically described their mounted colleagues as, "mere vampyres hanging on to the infantry – doing little fighting but first in for the spoils."

In the face of improved firepower the cavalry abandoned the sword for the hand gun or carbine. Carbines were shorter versions of the longarms of the day, their size making them stowable in a saddle holster and easier to handle in battle from the back of a horse. Less weight meant that they could be fired one-handed if necessary. The first

Men of Company I, 5th Ohio Cavalry proudly display their Sharps Carbines.

examples were muzzleloaders but these were soon replaced with breechloaders, while the best had a multiple shot capability.

As with all weapons in the Civil War, supply was less certain for the Confederate forces than for the Federal cavalry. Some supplies to the South came from less scrupulous Northern manufacturers whose desire for profit margins outweighed their patriotic tendencies by a good long way. And, of course, many units equipped themselves from weapons captured on the battlefield.

The Richmond Armory produced around 5,500 carbines whilst S.C. Robinson of Richmond, and subsequently the Confederate Government, produced around 5,000 weapons copied from the

Sharps design. Cook & Brother were another prolific Southern manufacturer, with their factories in Athens, Georgia, and New Orleans, Louisiana making about 1,500 carbines.

Other notable manufacturers included: G.W. Morse of Greenville, South Carolina, Bilharz, Hall and Company, Kean, Walker and Company, J.P. Murray, Read & Watson, Tallassee Armory and J.H. Tarpley.

The combined manufacture of the Southern armories came to around 18,000 carbines and was augmented by an estimated 5,000 British-made musketoons and cavalry carbines of the Enfield Pattern which managed to find their way through the blockades.

The Union made adequate provision for a supply of carbines relatively early on in the war by ordering significant quantities from a variety of different suppliers. At least seventeen different models were purchased, and here came the catch. The variety of ammunition calibers and types created problems for unit supply, especially where individual companies within the same regiment were issued with different weapons (a not uncommon occurrence).

A U.S.N. powder flask manufactured by N.P. Ames to match the 1847 Jenks carbine that was supplied to the Navy before and during the war.

A wooden ammunition crate which would have held 1,000 buck and ball cartridges for percussion rifle-muskets. A soldier would be issued with 40 rounds.

Individual designers had conceived their creations in isolation, while the government had not thought to stipulate sufficient standardization or interchangeability. For example, the Burnside carbine used a singular ice cream cone shaped .54 inch caliber cartridge whereas the Smith used a .50 inch caliber rubber cartridge.

The most successful and popular carbine of the war was the Spencer, and over 95,000 were purchased by the Federal Government during the course of the war. The Spencer used the No.56 copper rimfire cartridge in .52 inch caliber and combined rapid breechloading with multi-shot capability. It was closely followed by the single shot Sharps with its .52 inch caliber linen cartridge. Over 75,000 of these excellent guns were made.

Next in the "big five" was the Burnside with 53,000 units purchased, then the Smith with 31,000, and the Gallager with around 17,000.

Other notable manufacturers included Gibbs, Gwynn & Campbell, Joslyn, Lindner, Maynard, Merrill, Sharps & Hankins, Starr, Triplett & Scott, and Warner, while Remington manufactured the Jenks 'Mule Ear' carbine for the Navy.

Despite the troubles with supply and lack of standardization the carbine made its mark and the lesson of firepower being king was well and truly learned by both sides.

A lesson that was carried forward to all future combat zones.

Above: Don Troiani's painting "Last Rounds" depicts a Confederate unit reaching the end of their ammunition supplies in the heat of battle. The men are using Maynard Carbines, Enfield Carbines and Enfield 2-band Rifles.

Its external action and back-action lock plate hide the fact that this is a relatively modern weapon with a seven-shot repeating capability.

Ball Lever Action Carbine

Although this gun was delivered too late for action it is generally considered a Civil War weapon. Only 1,002 were made, having been contracted in 1864 by the federal Government, and they were delivered in May 1865, after the war finished. Manufactured by Lamson & Co., Windsor, Vermont, this is a seven-shot rimfire repeating arm, operated by a lever which doubles as the trigger guard. The left hand side of the receiver has a robust saddle-ring on a sliding lug (see inset detail). It has a two-piece walnut stock with a three-quarter length fore-end fastened by two barrel bands. The finish is casehardened brown with the standard six-line marking on the left side of the frame. The stock has an inspector's cartouche marked "GGS" on the left side.

The Bilharz, Hall and Co. Carbine shown with its breech block open and operating lever down.

SPECIFICATIONS

Type: breechloading percussion carbine

Origin: Bilharz, Hall and Company, Pittsylvania Courthouse, Virginia

Caliber: .54

Barrel Length: 21 in

The sling ring fixing was secured on a sliding bar.

SPECIFICATIONS

Type: repeating cartridge carbine

Origin: Lamson & Co., Windsor, Vermont,

Caliber: .50 rimfire

Barrel Length: 20.5 in

The Bilharz, Hall & Company Rising Breech Carbine

One of the rarest of the Confederate carbines, which has been attributed to the manufacture of Bilharz, Hall and Company of Pittsylvania Courthouse, Virginia, although previously known as the "D.C. Hodgkins" carbine. Only 100 were produced.

It fires a .54 caliber projectile with a paper cartridge, and the trigger guard lever is used to operate the vertically rising breechblock. It has a 21-inch barrel fastened by a single iron band.

The finish is casehardened brown steel and all fittings are cast iron including the buttplate. There is a sling ring on the left side of the receiver. The stock is one-piece walnut.

These guns are believed to be hand made and bear makers marks, serial number and inspector's cartouche ("P" over "C.S.") on barrel and breech.

The Colt Model 1855 Revolving Action appeared with different barrel lengths making it both a carbine and a rifle.

SPECIFICATIONS

Type: percussion revolver carbine

Origin: Colt Armaments Manufacturing Co, Hartford, Connecticut

Caliber: .36, .44 and .56

Barrel Length: 15 in, 18 in, 21 in and 24 in

Colt Model 1855 Revolving Carbine

A reasonably rare weapon that was produced in .36, .44 and .56 inch caliber and in barrel lengths of 15, 18, 21 and 24 inches. Only 4,435 were produced and their manufacture lasted from 1856–64. The .56 caliber version had a five shot cylinder and the .36 and .44 calibers were graced with six shots. This would have given the weapon a distinct advantage over single shot carbines of the day.

This one is a "British" type, with UK proof marks, and is a .56 caliber Standard Carbine with military finish but without the fore-end and bayonet lug that would characterize it as an Artillery Model. Markings on the top of the frame are "Col. Colt Hartford CT. U.S.A."

The left side of the frame has a lanyard ring and the stock is typically oil-stained walnut. The cylinder is fluted and stamped "Patented Sept 10th 1855".

Henry Kelly of the 1st Battalion, 1st Virginia Cavalry embraces his Colt Revolving Carbine.

The Second Model Burnside Carbine is characterized by the lack of a forend.

SPECIFICATIONS

Type: percussion breechloading carbine

Origin: Bristol Firearms Co., Bristol, and
    Burnside Rifle Co., Providence, both
    Rhode Island

Caliber: .54

Barrel Length: 21 in

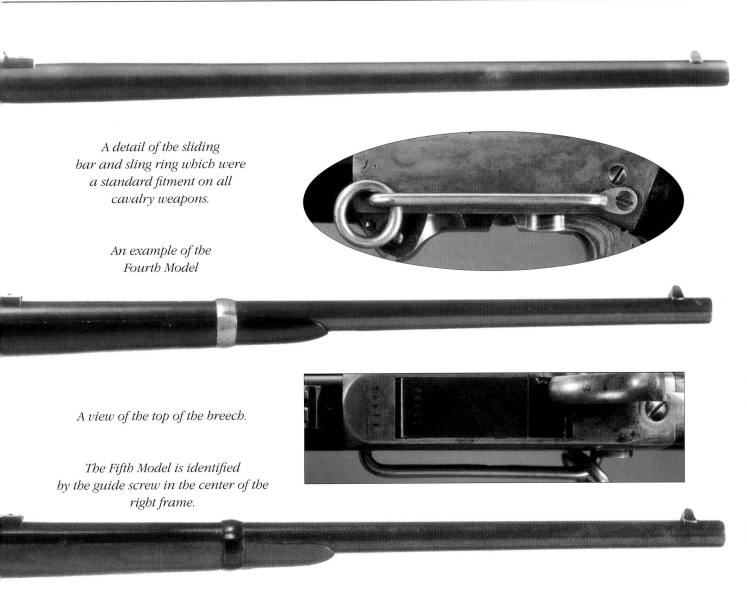

A *detail of the sliding bar and sling ring which were a standard fitment on all cavalry weapons.*

An *example of the Fourth Model*

A *view of the top of the breech.*

The *Fifth Model is identified by the guide screw in the center of the right frame.*

Burnside Carbine

A prolific series of Civil War carbines, the Burnside remained in production from 1857 to 1865. Designed by Ambrose E. Burnside, who at that time had formed the Bristol Firearms Co. in Rhode Island, it was later improved by one of his gunsmiths, George P. Foster. The company was also renamed the Burnside Rifle Co and moved to Providence, Rhode Island. After a faltering start, the carbine went on to great success, although most of that was after Burnside had sold his interests in the company. Burnside, of course, went on to greater things himself as the commander of the Army of the Potomac.

A short, lever-operated breechloading single-shot carbine, it used an unusual tapered cartridge cased with thin copper or foil, and had a tape primer system. The breech on the First Model is opened by a lever adjacent to the hammer, although fewer than 300 of these early examples were made in the years 1857–58.

The Second Model employs a catch inside the trigger guard to open the breech and is recognizable from later models by the lack of a fore-end stock. Two thousand were manufactured between 1860–62. The example shown is known to have been in action at Bull Run in July 1861 in the hands of a trooper from the

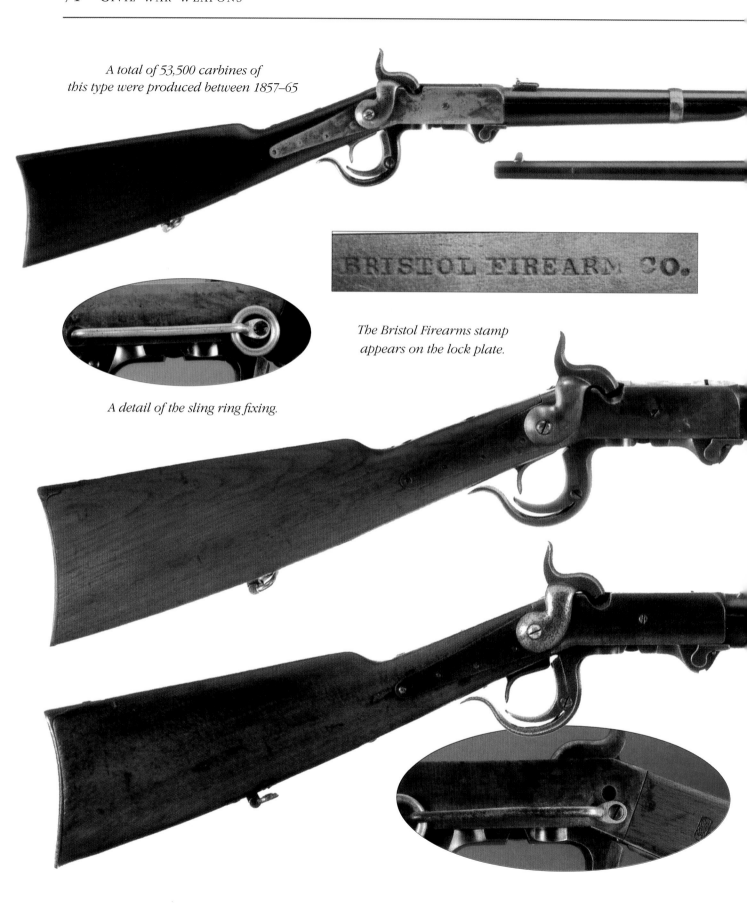

A total of 53,500 carbines of this type were produced between 1857–65

BRISTOL FIREARM CO.

The Bristol Firearms stamp appears on the lock plate.

A detail of the sling ring fixing.

*Detail, above right: Inspector's cartouche
from a Fourth Model.*

*Many fine examples have survived
from the long production run of the weapon.*

Rhode Island Infantry, a unit local to the factory. The Third Model used a similar breechblock to the Second model, but had a walnut fore-end and metal barrel restraining band.

The Fourth Model was produced between 1862 and 1864, and was marked as the Model 1863. It kept the barrel band and wooden fore-end of the Second Model, but employed a redesigned breech mechanism.

A hinged center section above the block allows for quicker and easier reloading. The Fourth Model can also sometimes be recognized by the lack of a guide screw on the right frame faceplate.

Another variant is marked as the Model of 1864, and is sometimes known as the Fifth Model. This version accounted for some 43,000 examples out of a total production run of 53,500 carbines, and are by far the most numerous of the weapons to be produced at the height of the Civil War. We show here details of the left and right sides of the frame and action, including the sliding saddle ring, the top of the breechblock and the inspector's cartouches. All finishes were originally blue.

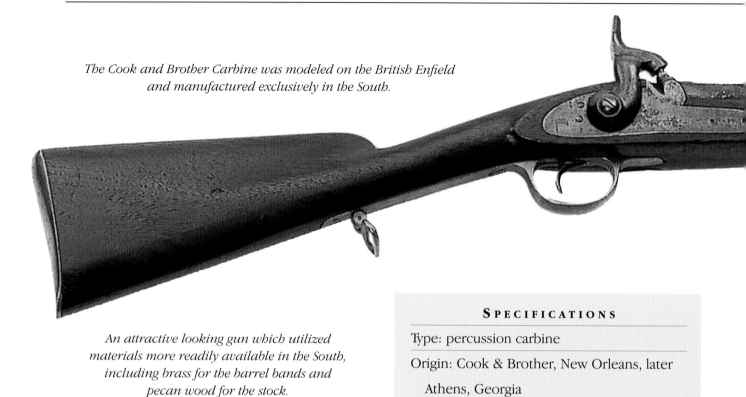

The Cook and Brother Carbine was modeled on the British Enfield and manufactured exclusively in the South.

An attractive looking gun which utilized materials more readily available in the South, including brass for the barrel bands and pecan wood for the stock.

SPECIFICATIONS

Type: percussion carbine

Origin: Cook & Brother, New Orleans, later
Athens, Georgia

Caliber: .58

Barrel Length: 21 in

Cosmopolitan Carbine

This forerunner to the Gwyn & Campbell Carbine was made in the same factory at Hamilton, Ohio. An order for 1,140 units for the State of Illinois was placed through the U.S Ordnance Dept. in December 1861 and delivered the following July. Virtually the whole batch was issued to the 5th and 6th Illinois Cavalry. The 6th Illinois Cavalry, commanded by Benjamin Grierson, took part in the spectacular "Grierson's Raid" in April–May 1863 when they roamed through the whole state of Mississippi, covering 600 miles in 16 days, which is a tribute to both the men and their equipment. The 5th Cavalry, who were issued with some 400 carbines, also saw much action in Arkansas and Mississippi.

The first 50 guns produced are recognizable by an enclosed lever extension of the trigger guard which activates the falling block action, whereas all subsequent production examples, known as the contract type, had a serpentine lever like the model shown. This one bears the marking "Hamilton O.,U.S. /Gross Patent".

Cook and Brother Carbine

A short carbine typical of the early Civil War period, where muzzleloading weapons were still very much in evidence. And as they had less industrial resources at their disposal, the Confederacy retained more muzzleloaders than did the federal army. America was seen as a great opportunity for foreign gunmakers, and two such were Ferdinand and Francis Cook, a pair of Englishmen who set up shop in New Orleans in 1860. They were in an ideal place to capitalize on the rapid demands of wartime production, and manufactured quantities of this cavalry carbine based on the Enfield pattern.

With the approach of Northern forces around 1862 they decamped to the relative safety of Athens, Georgia where production resumed from 1863–64. Over 1,500 guns of this type were produced. Stocks were either walnut or maple but some pecan wood is believed to have been used, being a close cousin to walnut and more readily available in the South. Furniture was brass with a cast iron ramrod with flat button tip operated by a swivel joint. It is generally reckoned that the Athens production models were better engineered than the earlier New Orleans models, but collectors will pay far more for earlier, more scarce, guns from the original factory.

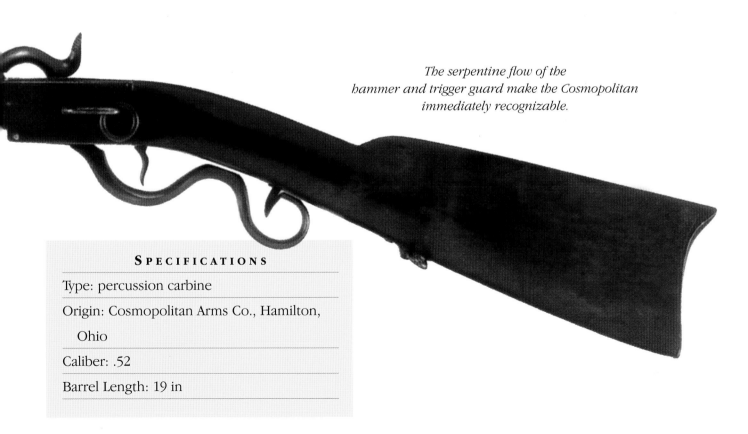

The serpentine flow of the hammer and trigger guard make the Cosmopolitan immediately recognizable.

SPECIFICATIONS

Type: percussion carbine

Origin: Cosmopolitan Arms Co., Hamilton, Ohio

Caliber: .52

Barrel Length: 19 in

SPECIFICATIONS

Type: muzzle-loading percussion carbine

Origin: Enfield, England and Tower
    Armouries, England

Caliber: .577

Barrel Length: 21 in

SPECIFICATIONS

Type: single-shot, cartridge carbine

Origin: Richardson & Overman, Philadelphia,
    Pennsylvania.

Caliber: .50

Barrel Length: 22.25 in

The Enfield Carbine was used by both sides, making it the most popular foreign carbine to see action in the war.

Enfield Pattern 1853 Cavalry Carbine

The British Enfield Pattern 1853 Rifle was by far the most popular foreign arm to be purchased during the Civil War, as both sides looked to overseas to make up the shortfall in their infantry weapons. Nominally .577 caliber, it could actually also fire the U.S. standard .58 Springfield ammunition.

Carbine versions of the Enfield were also made for cavalry and artillery issue. Using the same lock and mechanism of their larger brethren, they are distinguished by their short 21-inch barrels, two muzzle bands and a swivel ramrod. Many were also ordered by the Confederate States, although fewer than 5,000 of these carbines actually got through the blockade.

Two very different surviving examples of the Gallager Carbine. Many guns were converted into shotguns after the war.

Gallager Carbine

Designed by Mahlon J. Gallager from South Carolina, this gun was used extensively in the Civil War. Patented July 17, 1860, it continued in production at the Richardson and Overman factory in Philadelphia throughout the War. Nearly 18,000 units were made and surplus examples continued in civilian use for many years, either as rifles in .44 caliber or as shotguns. Several gun dealers, such as Bannerman's in New York, offered these conversions, giving credit to the basic reliability of the arm.

It was single shot breechloader in .50 caliber loaded by activating the trigger guard to slide the barrel forward allowing access to the breech. One early problem was the lack of an ejector for the spent cartridge but this was put right on later production when the gun was chambered for the Spencer .56-52 cartridge. The long iron patchbox was a small luxury which many other designs avoided in order to keep cost and production time down. Regiments known to have been equipped with the Gallager were the 2nd, 3rd, 4th and 6th Ohio, the 13th Tennessee and the 3rd West Virginia.

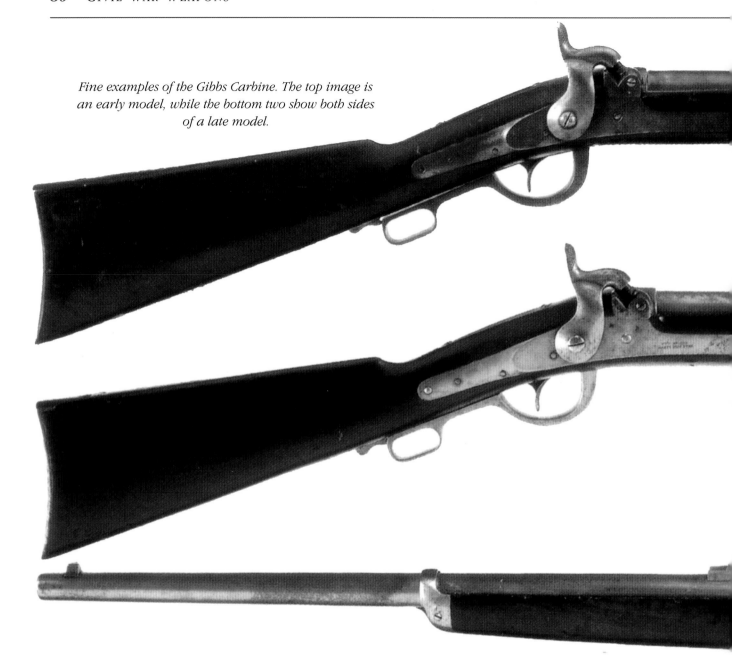

Fine examples of the Gibbs Carbine. The top image is an early model, while the bottom two show both sides of a late model.

Gibbs Carbine

Shown here are two of the rarest Civil War carbines to have survived. An order for 10,000 was placed by the federal government with the New York, Phoenix arms factory, owned by W. F. Brooks and W. W. Marsden. The factory was destroyed in the New York Draft Riots of 1863, at which time only 1,052 guns had been completed. The action is similar in operation to that of the Gallager with the barrel sliding forward to access the breech. Those guns that were actually completed were distributed to the 10th Missouri Cavalry, and the 13th and 16th New York Cavalry. Early models can be identified by "W.F. Brooks/Manfd. New York" (without the date) on the lock only, while later models were also marked on the breech with the inscription "L.H. Gibbs/Patd/Jany 8, 1856". We show both types.

*The Gibbs Carbine has a neat forend cap which cleverly
doubles as a fixing band for the barrel.*

SPECIFICATIONS

Type: breechloading percussion carbine

Origin: William F. Brooks, New York,
New York

Caliber: .52

Barrel Length: 22 in

*The late model Gibbs carbine
from the left side showing the
sling ring on its sliding bar.*

These two examples of the Greene Carbine with 22-inch barrel.

The carbine below has an 18-inch barrel which identifies it as one made for British use in the Crimean War then reputedly re-imported into the U.S. for the Civil War.

SPECIFICATIONS

Type: breechloading percussion carbine

Origin: Massachusetts Arms Co., Chicopee

Falls, Massachusetts

Caliber: .54

Barrel Length: 18 in and 22 in

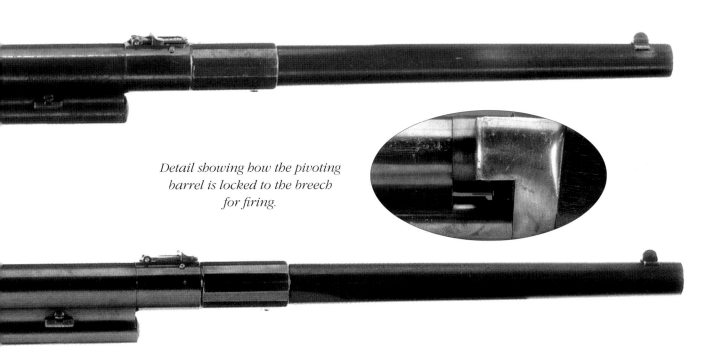

Detail showing how the pivoting barrel is locked to the breech for firing.

Greene Carbine

The original carbine was produced in limited quantities at the Chicopee Falls factory of the Mass-achusetts Arms Co. The gun is a .54 caliber single shot breechloader using the Maynard tape primer ignition system. The 22-inch barrel swung down and to the right to allow access to the breech, and the sling was mounted on the rear part of the trigger guard. Some 300 were made in this pattern and some are known to have been issued to the 6th Ohio Cavalry at the outbreak of the Civil War.

The other variant was the British Type Carbine easily distinguished by its 18-inch barrel and with the sling mounting half way down the underside of the stock. Two thousand of these were made for the British Government for use in the Crimean War but reputedly some of the surplus weapons were re-imported to the U.S. for use in the Civil War. One of the examples shown has "U.S." stamped on the stock near the buttplate, which would suggest military issue.

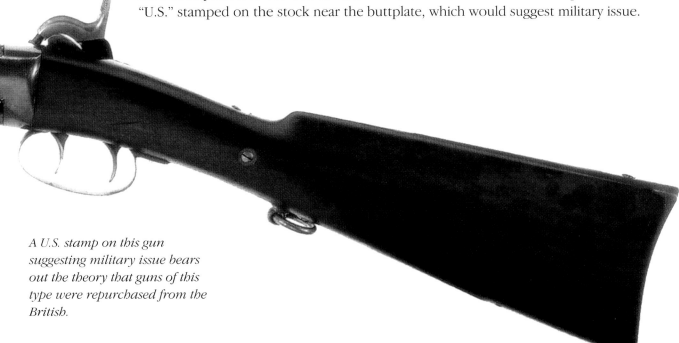

A U.S. stamp on this gun suggesting military issue bears out the theory that guns of this type were repurchased from the British.

*Over 4,000 Gwyn and Campbell
Type II Carbines were
manufactured.*

Gwyn & Campbell Carbine

Also known as the "Union Carbine" or the "Grapevine Carbine," this Civil War carbine was manufactured by Edward Gwyn and Abner C. Campbell of Hamilton, Ohio, and was the successor to the Cosmopolitan (see earlier entry). Made between 1863–64, 8,202 of these carbines were widely issued to the following Union Cavalry outfits: the 7th Tennessee, 5th and 8th Ohio, 4th and 8th Missouri, 3rd Wisconsin, 2nd and 3rd Iowa, 2nd and 3rd Arkansas, 5th, 6th and 16th Illinois, 2nd, 6th and 14th Kansas, and the 10th, 12th and 14th Kentucky.

Two distinct variants – the Type I and Type II – were produced in roughly equal numbers. The Type I (pictured top) has a spur at the tail of the trigger guard as the lever latch to operate the falling block action. The hammer and trigger guard are more exaggeratedly serpentine.

The Type II has a flatter hammer with a beveled edge and a more restrained trigger guard/lever. Standard markings include "Gwyn & Campbell", "Patent/1862/Hamilton/O." on the lockplate and "Union Rifle" on the left side of the receiver.

Above: An example of a Type I or Grapevine Carbine which can be easily identified by the more extreme curl of the trigger guard and hammer.

Detail of the lock plate of a Type II. The hammer has a flatter section.

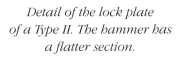

SPECIFICATIONS

Type: percussion breechloading carbine

Origin: Edward Gwyn and Abner C.
Campbell, Hamilton, Ohio

Caliber: .52

Barrel Length: 20 in

The fact that there is an obvious similarity between this gun and the Cosmopolitan Carbine can be explained as the guns came from the same factory.

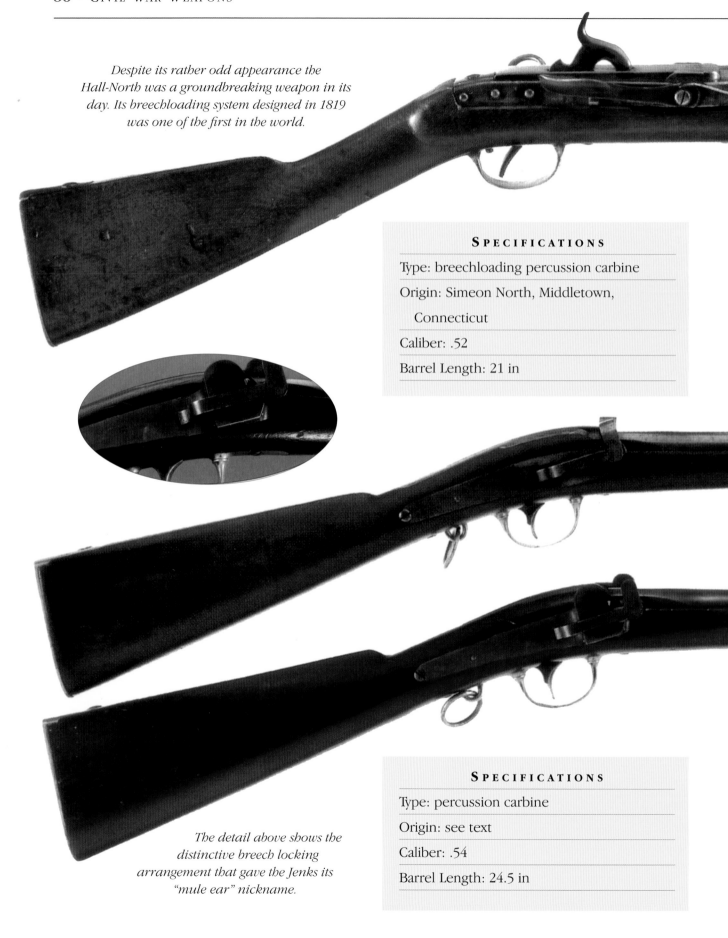

Despite its rather odd appearance the Hall-North was a groundbreaking weapon in its day. Its breechloading system designed in 1819 was one of the first in the world.

SPECIFICATIONS

Type: breechloading percussion carbine

Origin: Simeon North, Middletown,
    Connecticut

Caliber: .52

Barrel Length: 21 in

The detail above shows the distinctive breech locking arrangement that gave the Jenks its "mule ear" nickname.

SPECIFICATIONS

Type: percussion carbine

Origin: see text

Caliber: .54

Barrel Length: 24.5 in

Hall-North Carbine

John Hall's patented breech-loading system was used on the Model 1819 Rifle, and incorporated an unusual tip-up breech chamber, in which the breech-lock and chamber were incorporated into a single unit. Hall's mechanism was also used on cavalry carbines, and there were a range of models with minor variations in breech release lever and saddle ring bar. Originally made for flintlock ignition, as it was both rifles and a breechloader, it was seen as worth converting to percussion. Many later guns were made at the Harpers Ferry Armory but were generally identical to the 1819 model rifle excepting the distinctive "fishtail" breechblock release. The weapons shown here is a Model 1840, and was manufactured by Simeon North.

Two fine examples of the Jenks which saw service mainly with the U.S.N. and U.S. Revenue Cutter Service.

Jenks "Mule Ear" Carbine

The original model was designed by William Jenks who signed a contract with the navy in 1841 for the supply of a large quantity of his breech loading carbines. They were named "mule ear" because of the distinctive configuration of the breech lever and sidehammer, and were the only sidehammer type arm ever accepted by the U.S. armed forces. Jenks subcontracted supply to N.P. Ames of Springfield MA who were renowned for their excellent swords. Some 4,250 were produced between 1843–46, all of which went to the U.S.N. and U.S. Revenue Cutter service. In 1845 William Jenks signed a further contract with the U.S. Navy, this time to supply 1,000 of his carbines with Maynard Tape Primer locks, at which point Eliphalet Remington, after some negotiation with the proprietors of N.P. Ames, bought the contract to supply the guns. He also bought the machinery and had this shipped to the Remington plant. The subsequent production also benefited from another Remington improvement – the cast steel barrel. This gun is distinguished by the Remingtons/ Herkimer marking on the lock plate behind the Maynard primer box.

*We show three fine examples of
the Joslyn Carbine.*

*The Model 1864 can be most easily identified
by its steel barrel band.*

SPECIFICATIONS

Type: single-shot cartridge carbine

Origin: Joslyn Firearms Co., Stonington,
Connecticut

Caliber: .52 rimfire

Barrel Length: 22 in

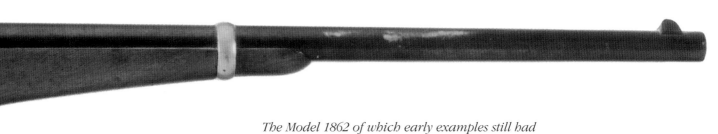

*The Model 1862 of which early examples still had
percussion ignition systems.*

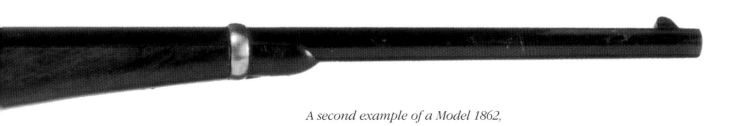

A second example of a Model 1862,

*Below are views of both sides of the lockplate
showing the sling ring and mount.*

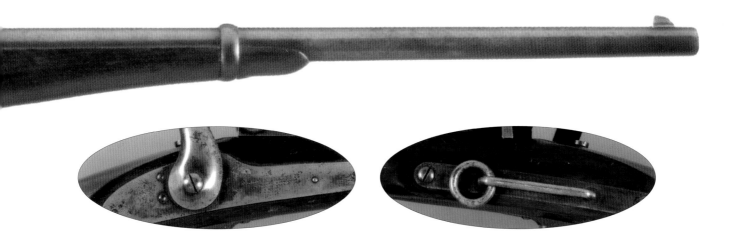

Joslyn Model 1862 and 1864 Carbines

The Joslyn turned out to be one of the most prolific of Civil War arms, being produced from early in the War through to spring 1865. It evolved during that time from percussion cap ignition to .52 rimfire ammunition in the early 1862 model, with the nipple giving way to the firing pin. Union Cavalry units equipped with the Joslyn were the 4th and 8th Indiana, 19th New York, 13th Tennessee, 9th Pennsylvania, 3rd West Virginia, 2nd Wisconsin, 1st Nebraska, 1st Nevada and 11th Ohio. Makers mark "Joslyn Firearms Co, Stonington, Conn." on the lockplate.

The Model 1862 accounted for about 3,500 of the total run of 16,500 and mainly differs in the style of the latch for the breechblock and an exposed firing pin extension. The later 1864 Model accounts for the bulk of the production, of which some 8,000 units were official Federal government purchase and 4,500 privately purchased through military outfitters like Schuyler, Hartley & Graham in New York

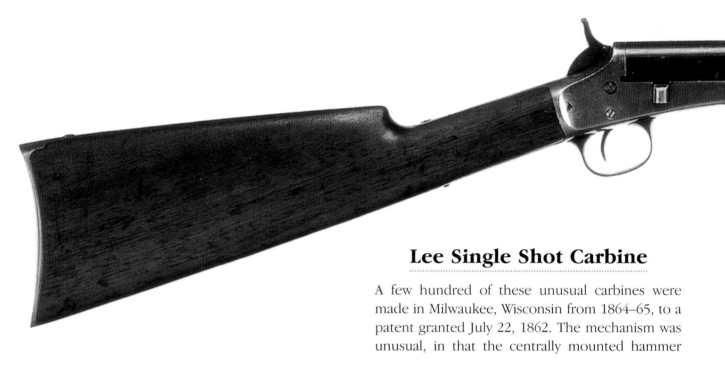

Lee Single Shot Carbine

A few hundred of these unusual carbines were made in Milwaukee, Wisconsin from 1864–65, to a patent granted July 22, 1862. The mechanism was unusual, in that the centrally mounted hammer

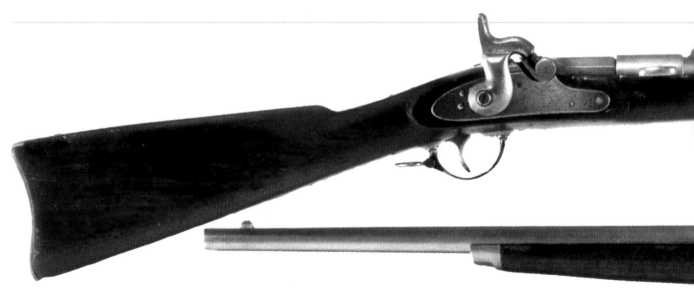

Lindner Carbine

This was a .58 caliber single shot breechloader operated by turning a sleeve on the barrel through 180 degrees, allowing the spring loaded breechblock to pop up ready for loading. The first type was produced in two contracts totaling 892 guns, and were marked "Edward Lindner's/ Patent /March 29, 1859" on the breech only. They were probably manufactured at the Amoskeag plant in Manchester, New Hampshire and were used by the 1st Michigan Cavalry and the 8th West Virginia Mounted Infantry.

A later contract from the Ordnance Dept to Amoskeag resulted in failure, in that 6,000 units were never inspected when completed and therefore ultimately rejected in 1864. Amoskeag fought an unsuccessful lawsuit and eventually had to sell the carbines off to the highest bidder. This was known as the Second Type and is shown here.

Above: The modern-looking Lee Carbine with its sleek integral hammer.

formed part of the barrel lock. When unlocked, reloading was achieved by pivoting the rear of the barrel out to the right. Ammunition was .44 rimfire. Very little information survives about the weapon other than a further order was placed for 1,000 and that the barrels, which were subcontracted to Remington, were produced in the wrong caliber leading to rejection of the order.

SPECIFICATIONS

Type: single shot cartridge carbine

Origin: Lee Firearms Co., Milwaukee,
   Wisconsin

Caliber: .44 rimfire

Barrel Length: 21in

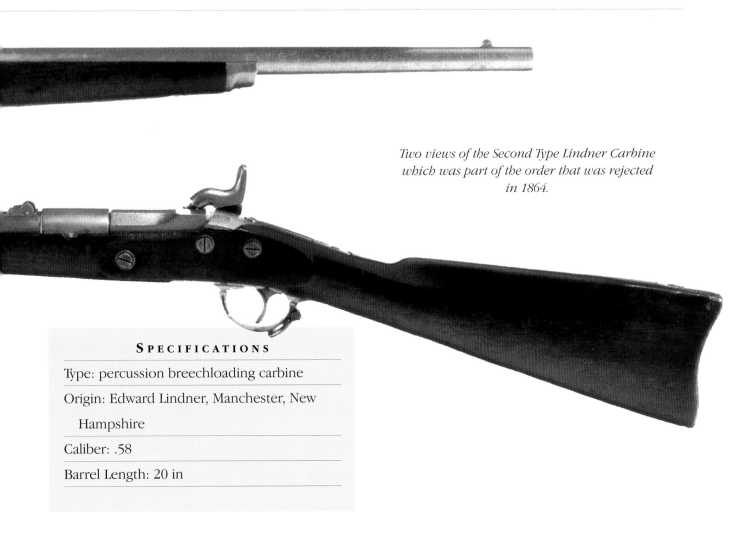

Two views of the Second Type Lindner Carbine which was part of the order that was rejected in 1864.

SPECIFICATIONS

Type: percussion breechloading carbine

Origin: Edward Lindner, Manchester, New
   Hampshire

Caliber: .58

Barrel Length: 20 in

All examples of the Second Model Maynard which had dispensed with the patent tape primer ignition.

The Second Model is identifiable by the deletion of the patchbox.

SPECIFICATIONS

Type: percussion, breechloading carbine

Origin: Massachusetts Arms Company, Chicopee Falls, Massachusetts

Caliber: .35 and .50

Barrel Length: 20 in

The Second Model saw service with the 9th and 11th Indiana and the 11th Tennessee Union Cavalry regiments

Maynard Carbine

Manufactured by the Massachusetts Arms Co. of Chicopee Falls, the gun was designed by Dr Edward Maynard, inventor of the tape primer ignition system which the weapon (and others) utilized. The Massachusetts Arms Company is worthy of mention in that many famous names are featured in the original board of directors of 1851, including Horace Smith and Daniel B. Wesson (later to form Smith and Wesson), Joshua Stevens (later J. Stevens Arms Co.) and J.T. Ames (Ames Mfg.Co.). The company was originally established in buildings that were part of the Ames plant and was intended to produce revolvers as a rival to Colt. However, the company entered the longarms market in 1855 with the manufacture of the Greene breechloading carbine, followed by the first Maynard Carbines in 1858–59.

The stamp on the left side of the frame shows clearly the manufacturer's name and location.

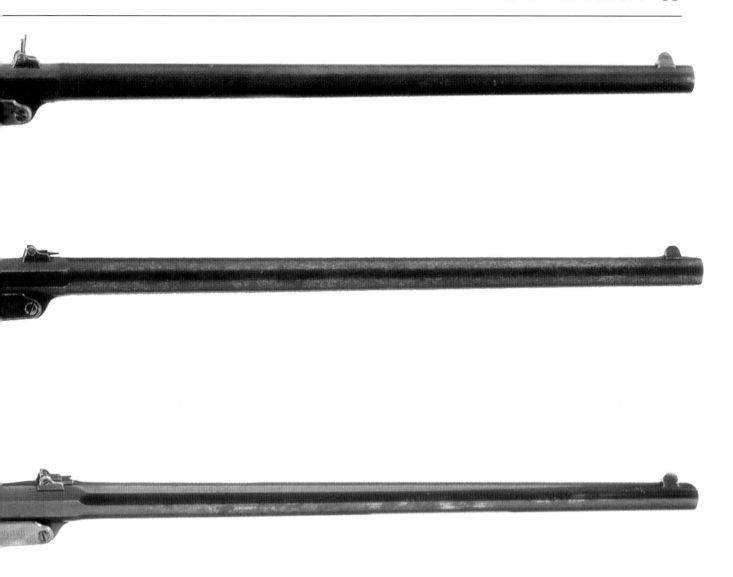

The company was dissolved in 1866 when wartime production shriveled away but was bought by T.W. Carter, the factory superintendent. It was taken over again in 1876 but its strong name and heritage was retained on each occasion.

The design of the Maynard Carbine led to the first Maynard sporting model rifles, which became the mainstay of the company's postwar business until 1890. The First Model carbine manufactured between 1858 and 1859 is easily identified by its patchbox in the stock. About 5,000 of these were made and were variously distributed to the 9th Pennsylvania and 1st Wisconsin, the U.S. Revenue service and to the Marines aboard the *U.S.S. Saratoga*. A large quantity was purchased by the Confederacy and the type was officially included in their ordnance manuals. The state of Mississippi purchased 325 carbines in .50 caliber and 300 in rarer .35 caliber. Florida took 1,000 in .35 and Georgia had 650 in .50 caliber. Some 800 were purchased by sundry militia outfits in South Carolina and Louisiana.

The vast majority of the output was of the Second Model, with over 20,000 manufactured between 1863–65 and known officially as the Model 1863. This model lacked the tape primer and the patchbox in the stock and is known to have been used by Union Cavalry units such as the 9th and 11th Indiana and the 11th Tennessee.

All of our featured weapons are from the Second Model production and are shown in various different states of preservation. All are .50 caliber.

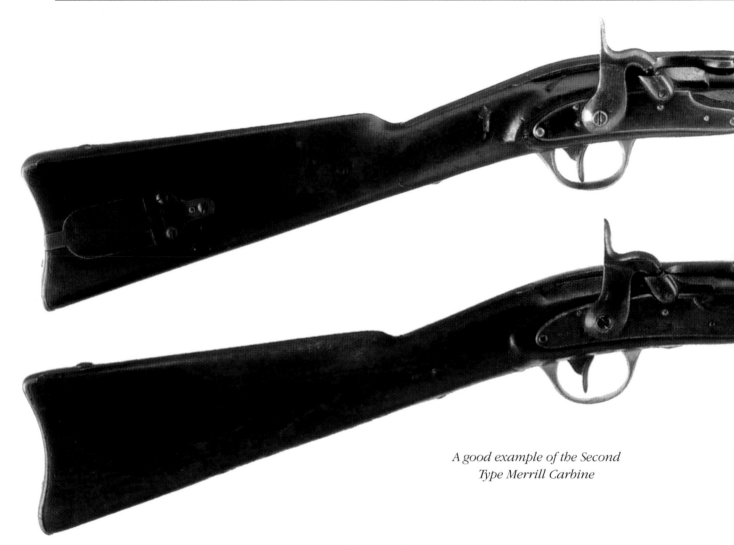

*A good example of the Second
Type Merrill Carbine*

Merrill Carbines

A simple and effective breechloader, a total quantity of 14,495 carbines were made by H. Merrill of Baltimore, Maryland. The majority of the production was accounted for by federal government purchase. Our top image shows the First Type, which had the patchbox in the butt.

Second Model production was inspired by the need to reduce manufacturing time and cost, which accounts for the patchbox not being present. There were other less apparent changes too, like the copper-faced breech plunger that sealed the percussion cartridge in the breech allowing less gas to escape. The Second Model also had modifications to the breech lever latch, making it a rounded button as opposed to a flat knurled type. There were variations in the sights and lockplates too. Union Cavalry Regiments known to have been issued with the Merrill were the 1st, 5th, and 18th New York, the 11th, 17th and 18th Pennsylvania, the 1st New Jersey, the 7th Indiana, the 1st and 3rd Wisconsin, the 27th Kentucky and 1st Delaware. The weapons shown are furnished with blued steel and bright brass.

SPECIFICATIONS

Type: percussion breechloading carbine

Origin: H. Merrill, Baltimore, Maryland

Caliber: .54

Barrel Length: 22.25 in

The First Type Merrill Carbine had a patchbox, but as with many other longarms, later models had these deleted as the war progressed. This was done to reduce costs and as ammunition evolved.

A box of five cartridges for the Merrill Carbine manufactured in Richmond.

*Two very well-preserved examples
of the Palmer Bolt Action Carbine.*

*The U.S. stamp shows
that weapons consignments had
been inspected.*

Palmer Bolt Action Carbine

W. Palmer patented the design of this breech-loading arm in December 1863, and Lamson were contracted to make them late in the Civil War with delivery being made in June 1865 after the fighting had stopped.

Only about 1,000 are known to have been manufactured although the carbine is significant in being the first metallic cartridge bolt-action weapons to be issued to U.S. troops. Despite this advanced feature the gun itself looks antiquated with a single banded wooden fore-end, traditional side hammer and lock, the hammer striking the cartridge rim to fire.

The bolt action mechanism is quite apparent in this model. A quarter turn of the toggle at the rear of the breech enables the bolt to slide back thus opening the chamber.

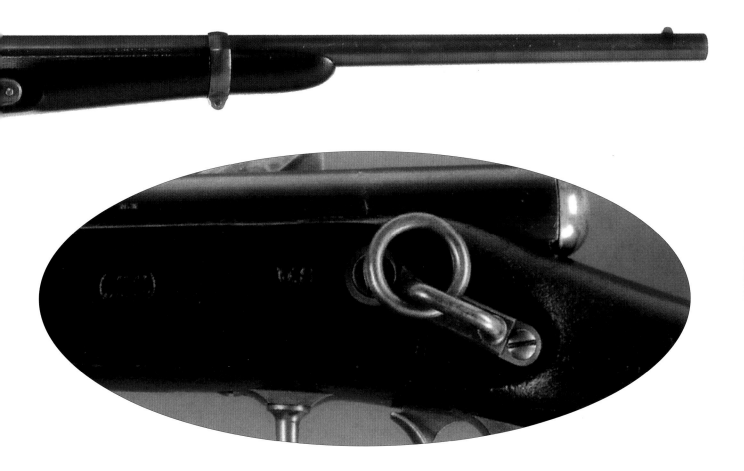

SPECIFICATIONS

Type: single shot bolt-action carbine

Origin: E.G. Lamson and Co., Windsor, Vermont

Caliber: .54 rimfire

Barrel Length: 20 in

The lockplate from the left side showing the sling ring arrangement.

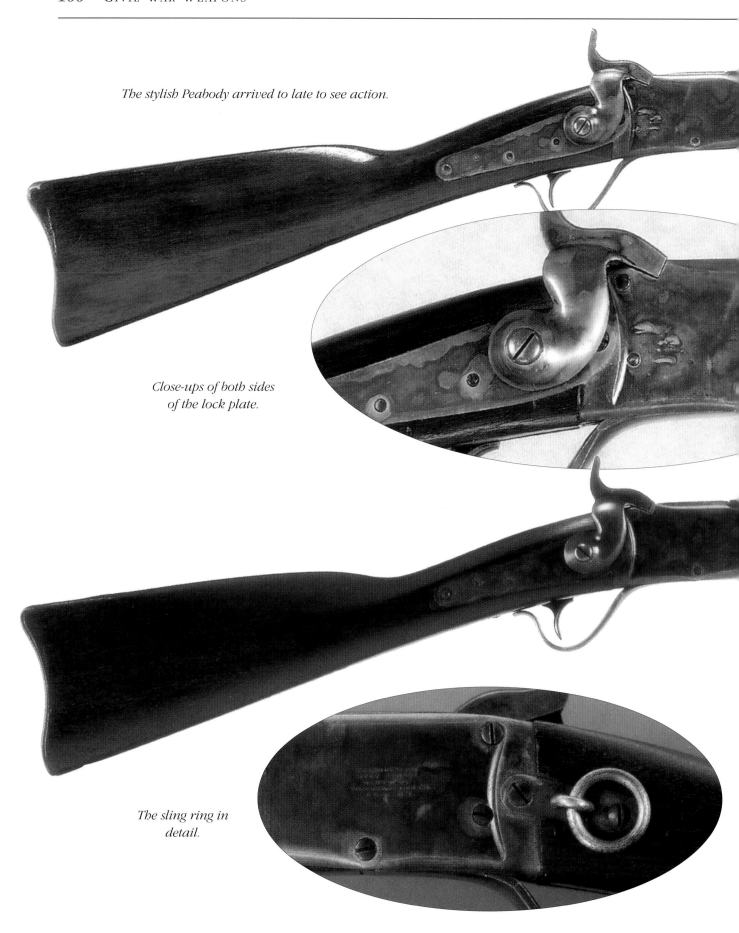

The stylish Peabody arrived to late to see action.

Close-ups of both sides of the lock plate.

The sling ring in detail.

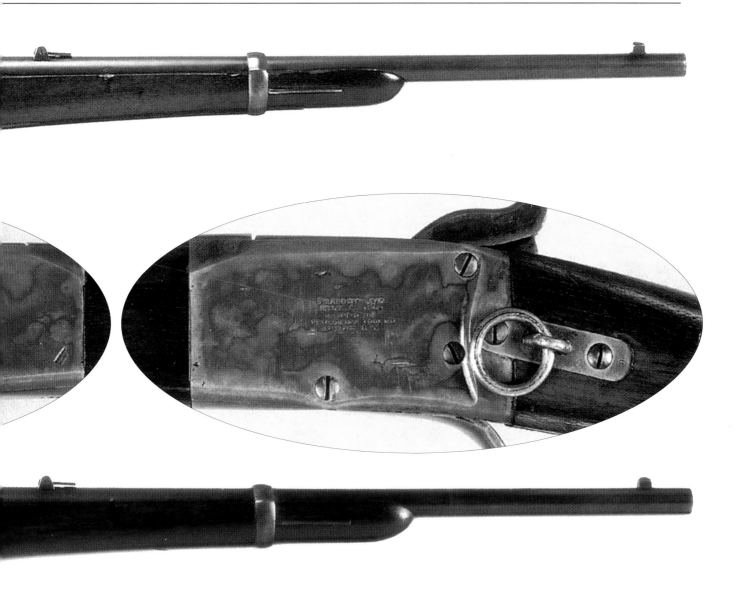

The Peabody was sold off in large numbers to foreign buyers, including 33,000 to France for use in the Franco-Prussian War.

Peabody Carbine

Developed during the Civil War, but ultimately arriving too late for service, the unfortunate Peabody was sold off to foreign powers such as Mexico, Canada, France and Spain. This meant that although all U.S. military interest ended with the war, the gun went on to provide its makers – The Providence Tool Company of Providence, Rhode Island – with a healthy income in the 1870s. Over 112,000 units, including the rifle version, of this fairly conventional rimfire breechloader were made.

SPECIFICATIONS

Type: breechloading percussion carbine

Origin: Peabody and Providence Tool
    Company, Providence, Rhode Island

Caliber: .50 rimfire

Barrel Length: 20 in

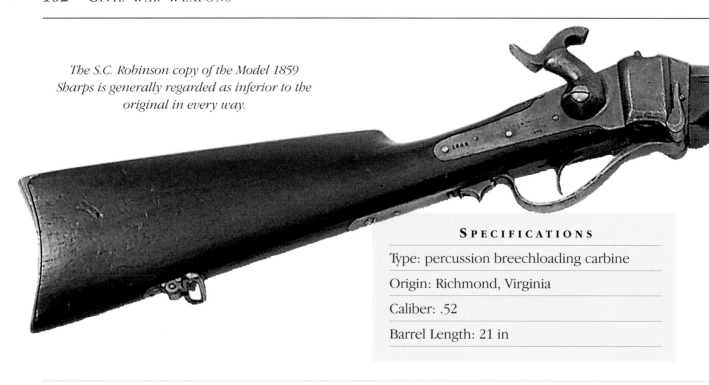

The S.C. Robinson copy of the Model 1859 Sharps is generally regarded as inferior to the original in every way.

SPECIFICATIONS

Type: percussion breechloading carbine

Origin: Richmond, Virginia

Caliber: .52

Barrel Length: 21 in

The Model 1852 can be identified by its "slanting breech."

The Model 1852 has a retaining spring embedded in the right rear section of the forend which disappeared on later models.

Sharps 1852 Saddle Ring Carbine

After working for other manufacturers, including John Hall at Harpers Ferry, Christian Sharps eventually set up his own company in 1851, in co-operation with Robbins and Lawrence, in Windsor, Vermont. Robbins and Lawrence made the weapons, while Sharps provided technical advice and marketed them from the Sharps Rifle Manufacturing Company, in Hartford, Connecticut. Sharps developed a range of single-shot breechloading rifles and carbines that were to be heavily used by soldiers in the Civil War and after, and also by sportsmen and hunters.

Other distinguishing features are the sling swivel which is attached to the underside of the buttstock, and the deleted patchbox.

Robinson Sharps Carbine

Made in Richmond, Virginia between 1862 and 1864 and based on the Hartford-made Model 1859 Sharps, this weapon generally lacked the refinement and quality workmanship of the original. Approximately 1,900 First Type guns were produced by Robinsons between 1862–63. The Confederate Government took over the Robinson factory in March 1863 and introduced the Second Type, which was identical to the First except for the markings on the breech ("Richmond, VA.").

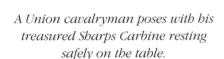

A Union cavalryman poses with his treasured Sharps Carbine resting safely on the table.

SPECIFICATIONS

Type: single shot, breechloading percussion carbine

Origin: Sharps Rifle Manufacturing Company, Hartford, Connecticut.

Caliber: .52

Barrel Length: 21.5 in

This is one of Sharps' earlier designs, and is a neat .52 caliber cavalry carbine which used the Sharps patent pellet primer mounted on the lockplate. It is recogn-izable from later models by the "slanting breech" on the side of the frame. The sling ring bar is unusual it that it extends from the breech to the barrel band. This often seems to have been repaired on surviving examples and perhaps the extra length subjected the part to stress. Some 5,000 units were manu-factured in serial numbers 2050–7500. Our two examples are early guns, being numbered in the 2600–3950 range.

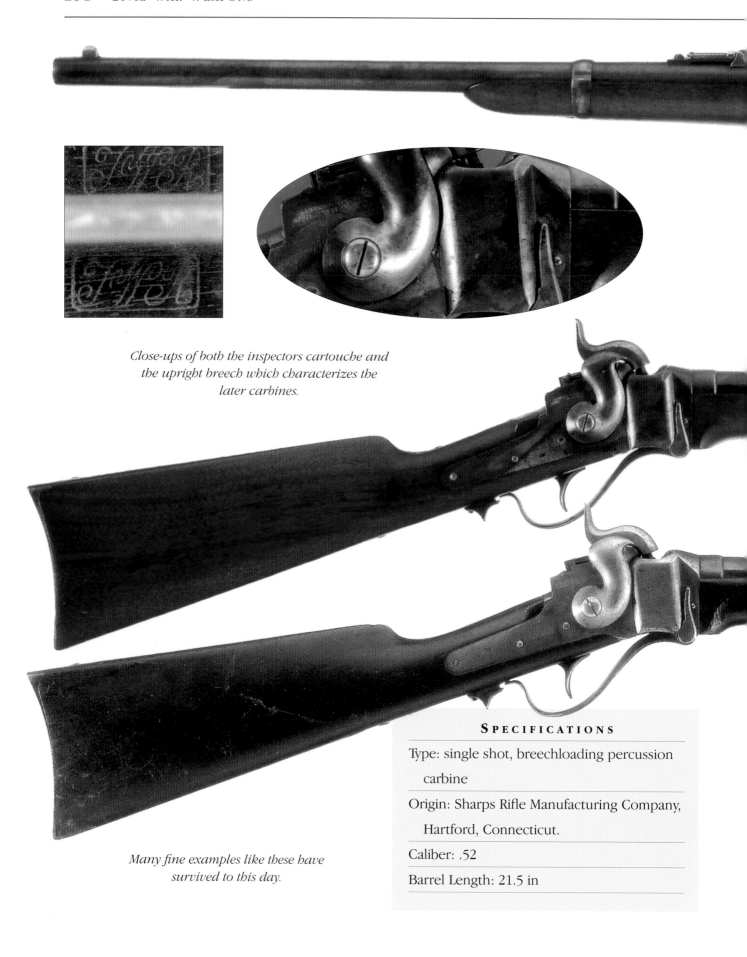

Close-ups of both the inspectors cartouche and the upright breech which characterizes the later carbines.

Many fine examples like these have survived to this day.

SPECIFICATIONS

Type: single shot, breechloading percussion carbine

Origin: Sharps Rifle Manufacturing Company, Hartford, Connecticut.

Caliber: .52

Barrel Length: 21.5 in

*The left side showing the sling
ring arrangement.*

*Both these guns are without patchboxes and with steel
furniture.*

Sharps New Model Carbines

As a result of experience with the Model 1852, the Sharps Company updated the design to what is known as the straight breech, or New Model rifles and carbines. As far as the carbine series goes, some 98,000 were made of Models 1859, 1863, and 1865, although they can be regarded as a single type. The Model 1863, which we are illustrating, was produced both with and without a patchbox (twice as many without). Both our examples are without.

The Sharps pellet priming system is now integral with the lockplate, the furniture is now iron including the cast barrel band, and the sling ring bar on the left side of the receiver is shorter, extending rearwards to the middle of the wrist. Most of the output was put in the hands of federal troops, but the State of Georgia managed to acquire 2,000 for its cavalry and infantry from the first production of the 1859 model, the only batch to retain brass furniture. Ironically, by the time these successful weapons had been developed, Christian Sharps had severed all association with the company, and by 1854 had formed a new partnership with William Hankins (see below).

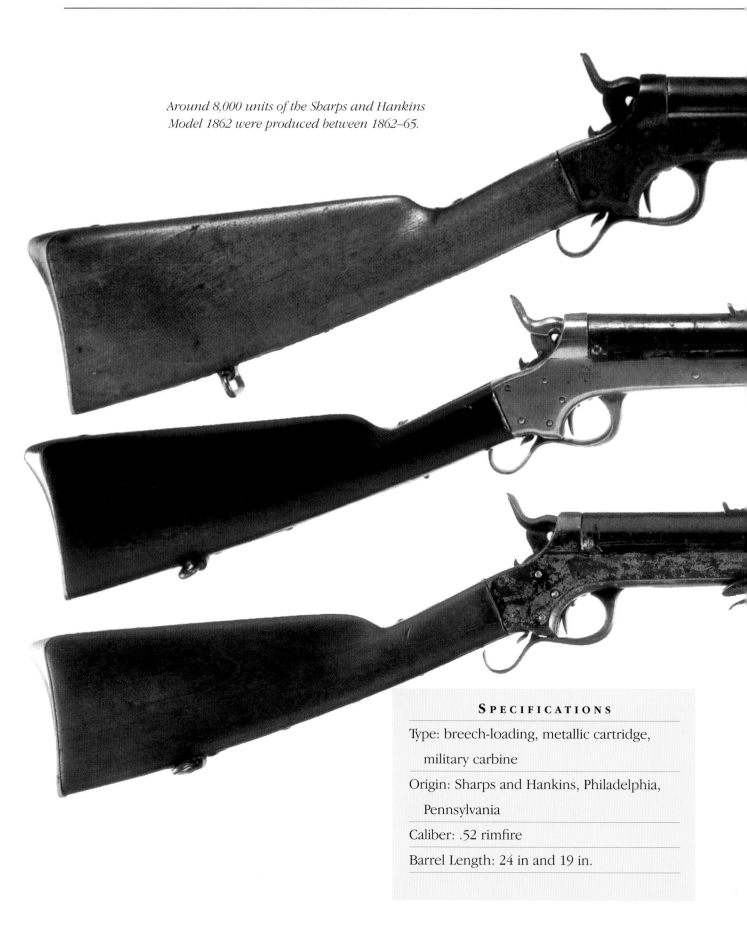

Around 8,000 units of the Sharps and Hankins Model 1862 were produced between 1862–65.

SPECIFICATIONS

Type: breech-loading, metallic cartridge,
   military carbine

Origin: Sharps and Hankins, Philadelphia,
   Pennsylvania

Caliber: .52 rimfire

Barrel Length: 24 in and 19 in.

*The Cavalry Model with a 19 inch barrel was issued to
the 11th New York Volunteers.*

*The Navy Type has a 24-inch barrel covered with a leather
sleeve to prevent corrosion. This is usually in a bad way but
looks in good condition on the lower example.*

Sharps & Hankins Model 1862 Carbine

In 1853 Christian Sharps was no longer associated with the Sharps Rifle Manufacturing Company in Hartford, Connecticut. He returned to Philadelphia and set up as C. Sharps & Company and set about manufacturing a breechloading, single shot pistol. In 1862 he formed a partnership with William Hankins to produce weapons for the Civil War, and began manufacture of this sliding barrel action carbine. A total of 8,000 were made between 1862–65.

Production was mainly centered on the navy type, which had the unusual feature of a leather-covered barrel to prevent corrosion. This has not stood the test of time particularly well and many surviving examples have the leather in poor condition. An army type was made in small numbers (around 500) and which lacked the fixings for the leather barrel sleeve.

There was also a cavalry carbine, with a shortened 19-inch barrel and saddle ring. This weapon was used by the 11th New York Volunteer Cavalry and is often known by that name. Confusingly many surviving examples still bear the Navy inspector's markings "P/HKH" despite being issued to the cavalry

Detail of the Inspector's cartouche stamped on the forend.

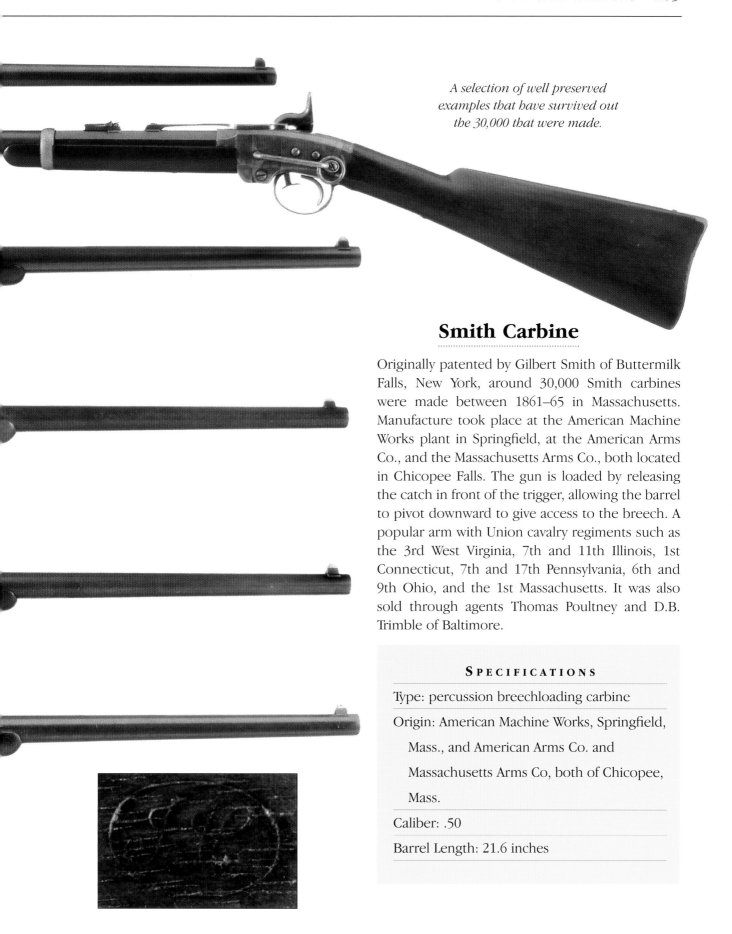

A selection of well preserved examples that have survived out the 30,000 that were made.

Smith Carbine

Originally patented by Gilbert Smith of Buttermilk Falls, New York, around 30,000 Smith carbines were made between 1861–65 in Massachusetts. Manufacture took place at the American Machine Works plant in Springfield, at the American Arms Co., and the Massachusetts Arms Co., both located in Chicopee Falls. The gun is loaded by releasing the catch in front of the trigger, allowing the barrel to pivot downward to give access to the breech. A popular arm with Union cavalry regiments such as the 3rd West Virginia, 7th and 11th Illinois, 1st Connecticut, 7th and 17th Pennsylvania, 6th and 9th Ohio, and the 1st Massachusetts. It was also sold through agents Thomas Poultney and D.B. Trimble of Baltimore.

SPECIFICATIONS

Type: percussion breechloading carbine

Origin: American Machine Works, Springfield, Mass., and American Arms Co. and Massachusetts Arms Co, both of Chicopee, Mass.

Caliber: .50

Barrel Length: 21.6 inches

Probably the most evocative Civil War gun and one which was personally endorsed by President Lincoln.

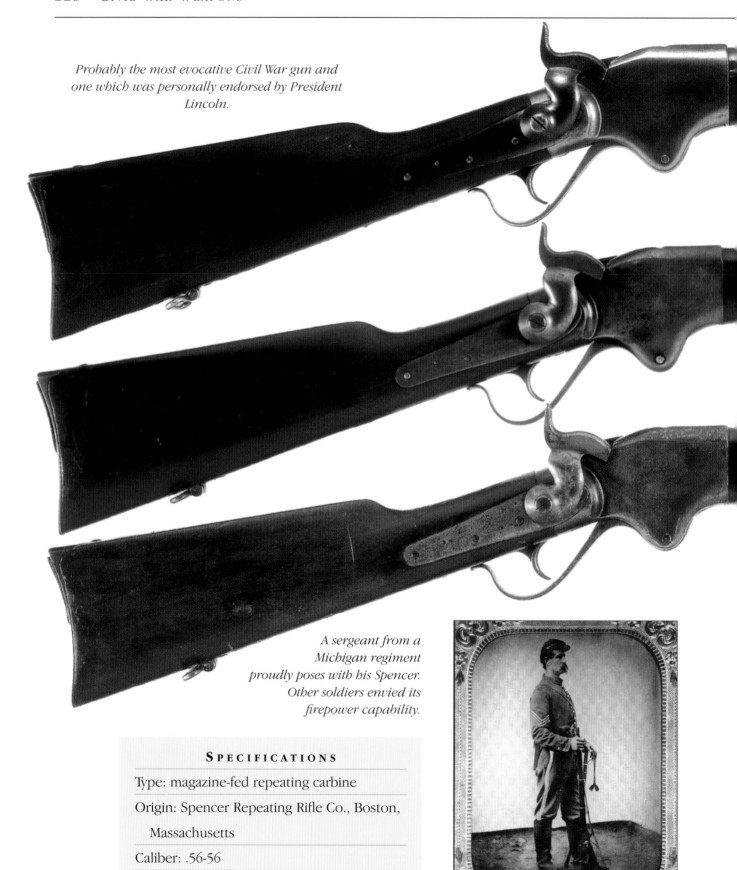

A sergeant from a Michigan regiment proudly poses with his Spencer. Other soldiers envied its firepower capability.

SPECIFICATIONS

Type: magazine-fed repeating carbine

Origin: Spencer Repeating Rifle Co., Boston, Massachusetts

Caliber: .56-56

Barrel Length: 22 in

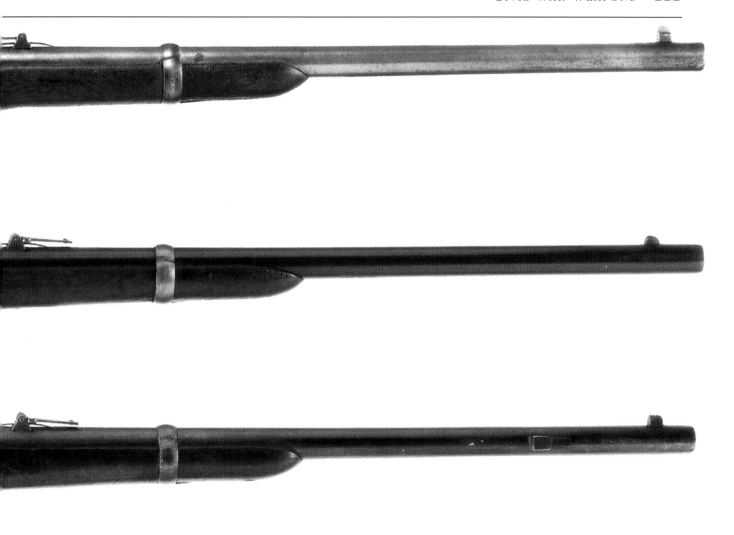

Spencer Repeating Carbine

Christopher M. Spencer initially made his weapons at South Manchester, Connecticut, until moving to Boston in about 1862. By that time he had already designed a successful repeating rifle and carbine, the latter of which is described here. This gun was definitely one of the most charismatic, successful and instantly recognizable weapons of the Civil War, and was so well received that it was personally endorsed by President Lincoln after he witnessed a field trial.

The gun is loaded via a tubular magazine housed in the buttstock, and rounds are fed into the breech by cranking down the trigger guard lever. Many soldiers were also equipped with the Blakeslee Cartridge Box, a wooden box containing between 6 and 13 metal tubes pre-loaded with 7 rounds. By placing the end of the reloading tube against the open end of the tubular magazine and dropping the cartridges through, the carbine could be reloaded in a matter of seconds.

The Spencer fired a .52 caliber rimfire straight copper cartridge. The case was actually .56 inches in diameter, so the cartridge is often referred to as the No. 56 or the .56-56.

We show several original examples of the 1860 and 1861 models. In an age when many of the troops on the opposing side still carried muzzleloaders, consider the advantages of being issued with a 7-shot repeating weapon. One Confederate Soldier captured at Gettysburg by Custer's Spencer-armed 5th Michigan Cavalry exclaimed, "[Spencers] load in the morning and fire all day."

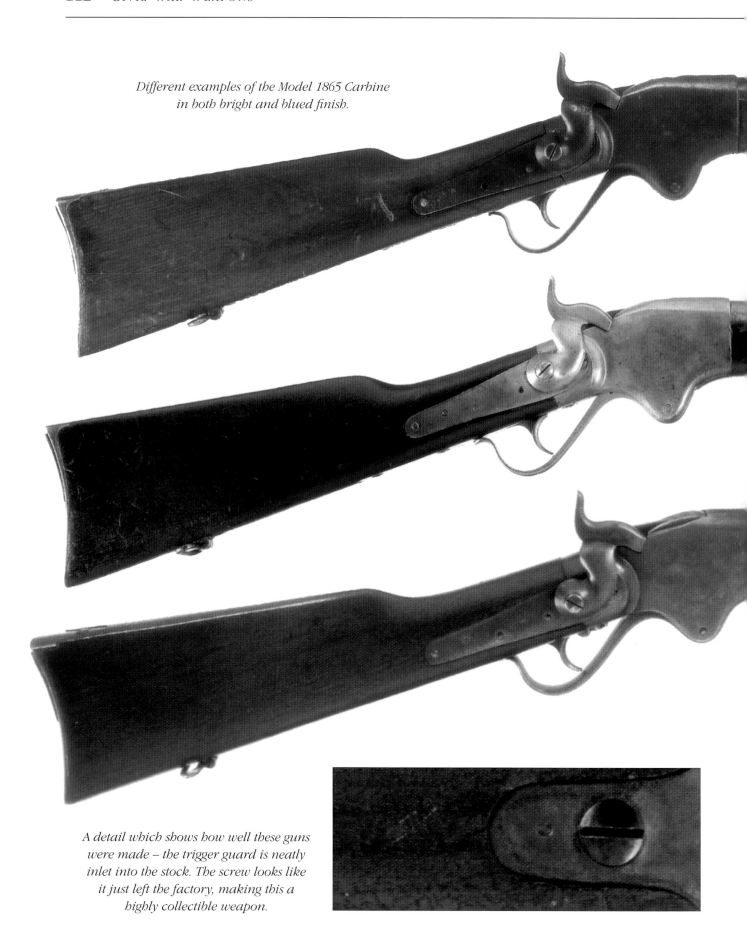

*Different examples of the Model 1865 Carbine
in both bright and blued finish.*

*A detail which shows how well these guns
were made – the trigger guard is neatly
inlet into the stock. The screw looks like
it just left the factory, making this a
highly collectible weapon.*

*This gun has the addition
of a sling swivel on the forend
band, a feature more commonly
seen on the rifle version.*

Spencer Model 1865 Carbine

Spencer also produced a later Model 1865, chambered for a .50 cartridge and with a slightly shorter 20-in barrel. Many were also fitted with the Stabler cut-off, a device which blocked the magazine. If careful, aimed, fire was needed, the user could block the magazine and feed single cartridges in to the breech, one at a time. The magazine could thus be kept full until rapid fire was needed, whereupon the firer simply slid the cut-off aside and let loose. Spencers continued to be used in the Indian Wars and on the Frontier for many years after the Civil War.

SPECIFICATIONS

Type: magazine-fed repeating carbine

Origin: Spencer Repeating Rifle Co., Boston, Massachusetts

Caliber: .50

Barrel Length: 20 in

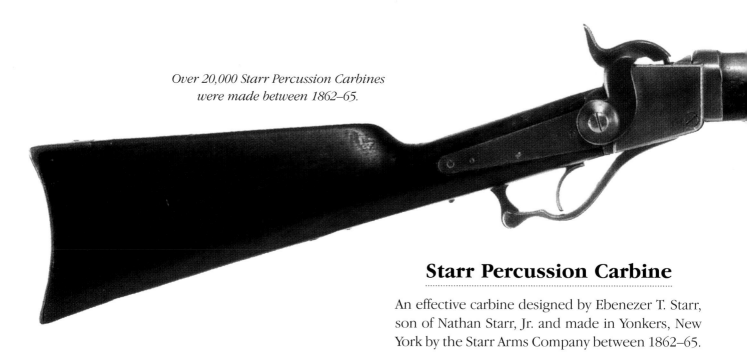

Over 20,000 Starr Percussion Carbines were made between 1862–65.

Starr Percussion Carbine

An effective carbine designed by Ebenezer T. Starr, son of Nathan Starr, Jr. and made in Yonkers, New York by the Starr Arms Company between 1862–65.

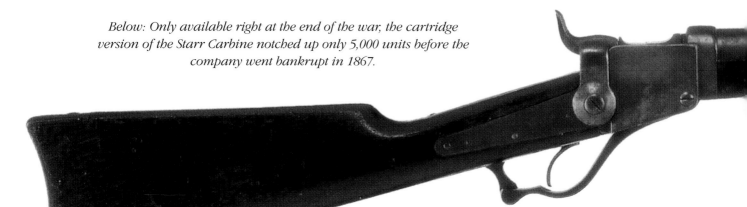

Below: Only available right at the end of the war, the cartridge version of the Starr Carbine notched up only 5,000 units before the company went bankrupt in 1867.

Starr Cartridge Carbine

This carbine used .52 caliber rimfire ammunition but was entirely similar to its percussion predecessor except for a less serpentine hammer. Timing was unfortunate, in that the final delivery of the 5,000 units made came right at the end of the Civil War, two weeks after Jefferson Davis had been captured by Union Cavalry.

As with so many other companies that had relied on wartime production for their livelihood, the return to peacetime spelled the end of the Starr Arms Co. and they went out of business in 1867.

SPECIFICATIONS

Type: cartridge carbine

Origin: Starr Arms Company, Yonkers, New York

Caliber: .52 rimfire

Barrel Length: 21 in

The weapon features a pull down trigger guard/lever to open the breech, single brass barrel band and walnut stock without patchbox. In government tests this gun came out ahead of the Sharps, although this was certainly not reflected in the ordering pattern: 20,000 of the Starr against nearly 100,000 for the Sharps. Union Cavalry regiments known to have used the Starr were the 1st Arkansas, 5th Kansas, 11th Missouri and 24th New York.

SPECIFICATIONS

Type: percussion carbine

Origin: Starr Arms Company, Yonkers, New York

Caliber: .54

Barrel Length: 21 in

Union troops with their Spencer Carbines.

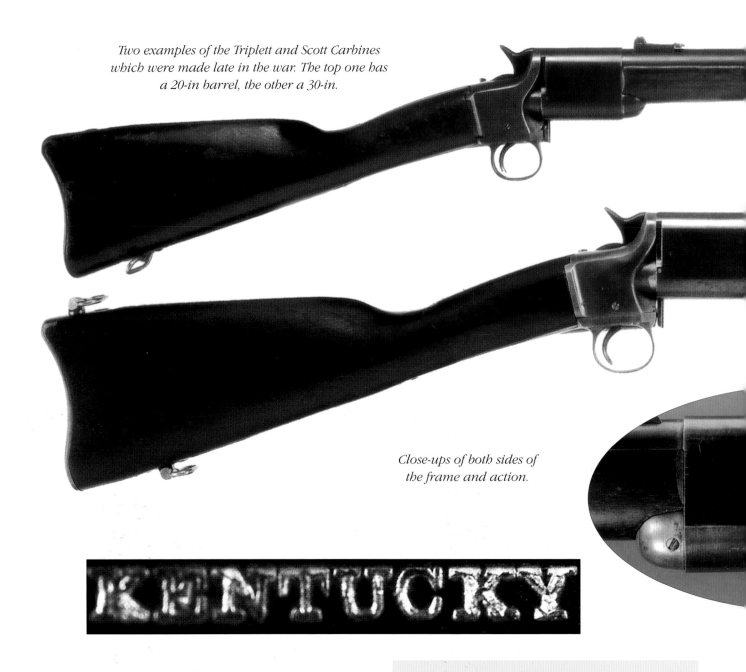

Two examples of the Triplett and Scott Carbines which were made late in the war. The top one has a 20-in barrel, the other a 30-in.

Close-ups of both sides of the frame and action.

The Kentucky stamping identifies this gun as part of the order for the Home Guard Troops in the State of Kentucky who were detailed to protect Sherman's supply lines during the Atlanta Campaign in 1865.

SPECIFICATIONS

Type: magazine-fed, repeating rifle and carbine

Origin: Meriden Manufacturing, Meriden, Connecticut

Caliber: .50 Spencer

Barrel Length: 20 in and 30 in

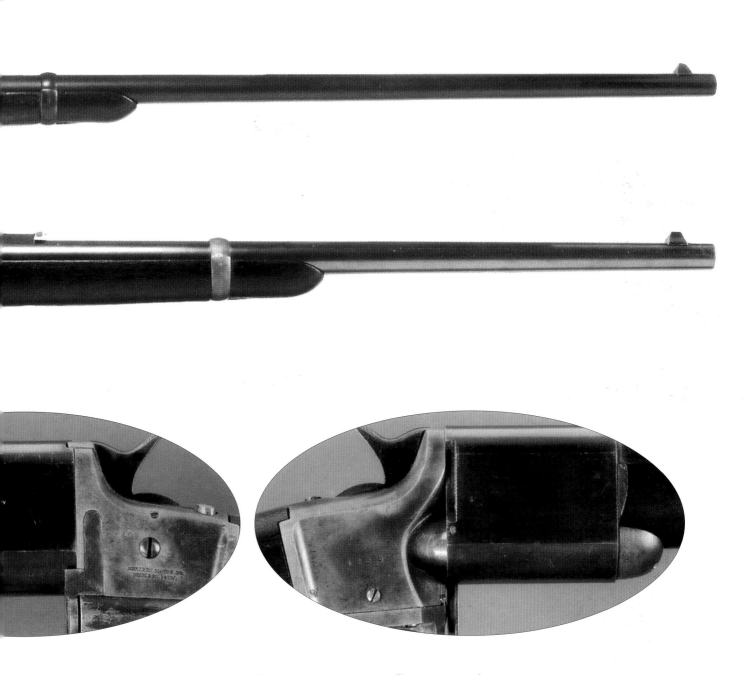

Triplett & Scott Rifle & Carbine

Louis Triplett of Columbia, Kentucky, and a co-worker named Scott were awarded a patent in December 1864 for a "magazine or self-loading fire-arm." As a result, their home state of Kentucky placed an order for 5,000 of these rifles which were made by the Meriden Company. They were intended for the Kentucky Home Guard who were protecting the supply lines of Sherman's Union Army, and most surviving examples are stamped "Kentucky" on the left side of the barrel frame.

Unfortunately the gun was too late to see active service in the Civil War. The two examples shown here are both chambered for the .50 Spencer round, but one has a 22-inch barrel and the other a 30-inch barrel. The Triplett & Scott system was unique and consisted of a barrel assembly which rotated to the right to load from a 7-shot tubular magazine in the butt-stock. As far as is known no other orders were placed and this somewhat complicated solution to the repeater rifle requirement was not pursued further.

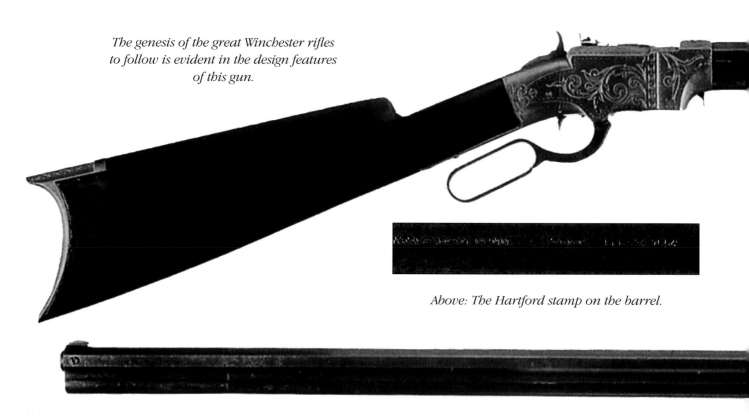

The genesis of the great Winchester rifles to follow is evident in the design features of this gun.

Above: The Hartford stamp on the barrel.

Percussion caps for the British Enfield together with an oiler bottle. Small service items such as these were an essential part of every soldier's kit.

*The fancy engraving on the brass receiver of
this gun indicates that it was a self-purchase rather than military issue.
This was an option for the better off soldier on both sides.*

New Haven Volcanic Rifle

The Volcanic company was formed in 1855 by Horace Smith and Daniel Wesson, but the former resigned later in 1855 and Wesson shortly afterwards. Oliver Winchester acquired the company's assets in 1857 and renamed it the New Haven Arms Company, which title it retained until 1866, when it became the Winchester Repeating Arms Company. A lever-action carbine was introduced during this period and sold in various calibers, barrel lengths and finishes. The example seen here is a carbine in the deluxe category with nicely engraved metalwork and a good quality walnut stock. The heavy octagonal barrel is 21 inches long. There are simple iron sights; a plain blade above the muzzle and a rather elementary adjustable rearsight on the receiver.

SPECIFICATIONS

Type: tubular magazine, repeating rifle

Origin: New Haven Arms Company, New
    Haven, Connecticut

Caliber: .41

Barrel Length: 21 in

This model was produced both by Greene and Warner. The eye-bolt sling ring attachment identifies this as a Warner produced gun.

Identification stamping on the trigger guard may have been made by the gun's original owner.

Warner Carbine

James Warner patented this breechloader in 1863, and it entered production with the Massachusetts Arms Co. in 1864. Only 1,500 of this simple but effective single shot weapon were produced. Brass frames always make for an eye-catching gun and this one is no exception. The breech is accessed by lifting the hinged block and extraction is by a slide at the rear underside of the forestock. There is a single saddle ring without a sliding bar.

SPECIFICATIONS

Type: breechloading cartridge carbine

Origin: Massachusetts Arms Co., Massachusetts

Caliber: .50 rimfire

Barrel Length: 20 in

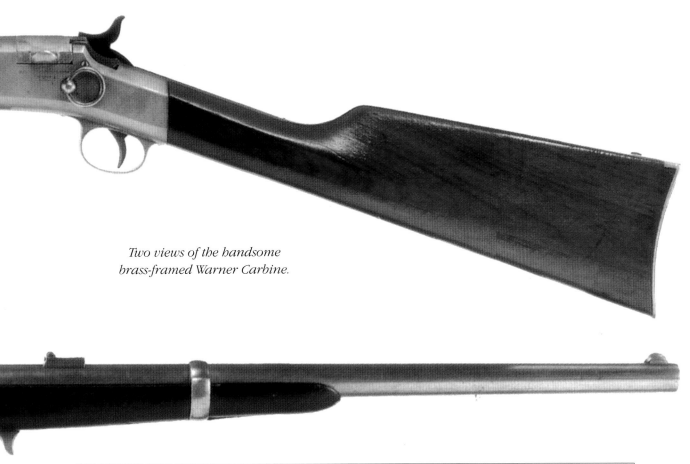

*Two views of the handsome
brass-framed Warner Carbine.*

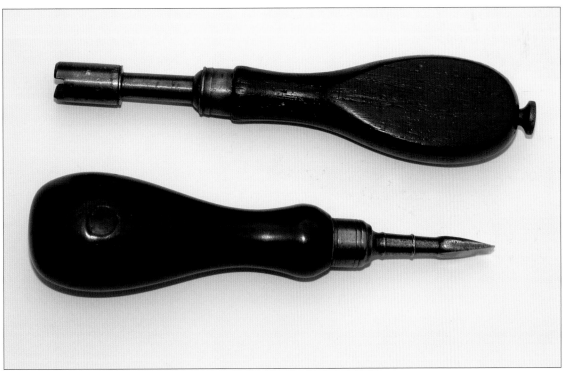

*Civil War-period nipple wrench and screwdriver. Both
essential tools for the battlefield.*

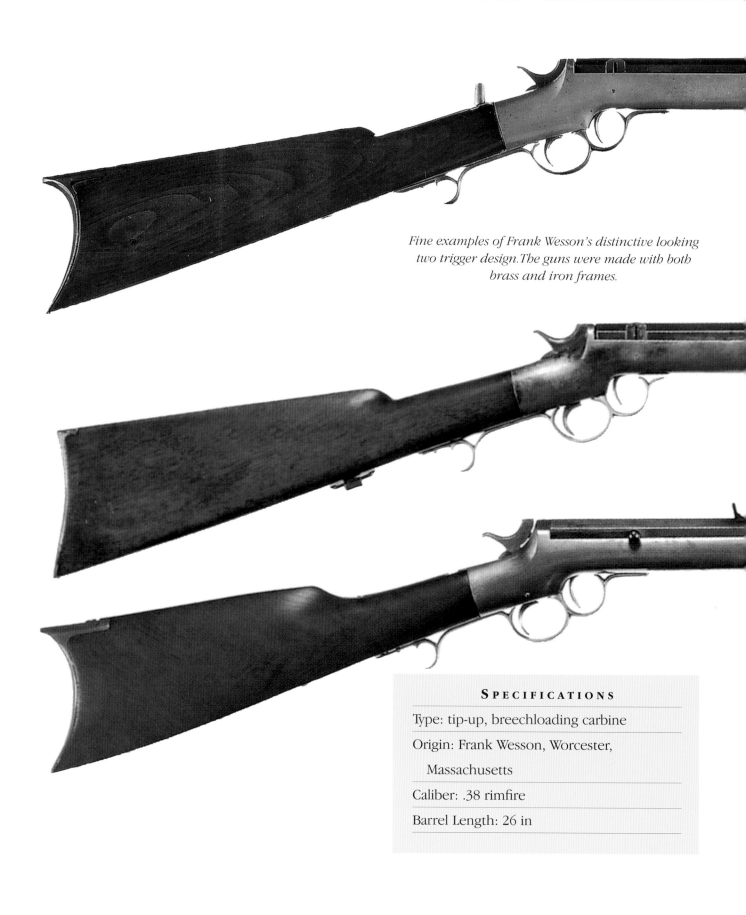

Fine examples of Frank Wesson's distinctive looking two trigger design. The guns were made with both brass and iron frames.

SPECIFICATIONS

Type: tip-up, breechloading carbine

Origin: Frank Wesson, Worcester,
   Massachusetts

Caliber: .38 rimfire

Barrel Length: 26 in

Frank Wesson Military Carbine

Frank Wesson was the brother of Daniel and Edwin and uncle to Edwin Wesson, all of whom made their names in the gun trade. He had a small gunmaking business in Worcester, Massachusetts where he made rifles and pistols for the civilian market, including the two-trigger, single-shot sporting rifle seen here, with a 26-inch barrel and chambered for .38 rimfire.

A tip-up, breechloading weapon, this was one of the first to use a metal cartridge case. Early models lacked an extractor, and when the rimfire cartridges occasionally expanded unduly in the breech, the spent cartridges had to be removed by fingers, often with the aid of a ramrod. A blade front sight, folding leaf back sight and sling swivels were standard on the carbine version.

Shown here is a Frank Wesson Two-Trigger rifle with a full octagonal, 26-inch barrel, and chambered for .38 Rimfire, which was presented, together with a saber, to Captain Joseph Walker, an extremely courageous officer of the United States 1st New York Engineer Corps. Walker's presentation saber can be seen on page 248.

CHAPTER THREE

Rifles and Longarms

When the young men of America flocked to the colors of both sides, they found themselves equipped with a bewildering array of weapons, supplied by a range of manufacturers from both the home country and from abroad. Armories and military stores had been scoured for weapons, purchasing agents roamed the world, independent contractors sprang up all over the country, while many men even brought along their personal pistols, revolvers and shotguns. The weapons described in this chapter show something of this panoply of designs, and include the obsolete, the unusual and the startlingly modern, as well as the widely-used "standards."

While both sides tried to standardize on types and calibers, it was never possible to do this fully. This was especially true in the case of the Confederacy, with their lack of industrial resources, and whose soldiers had to make the best of a huge variety of types, of varying degrees of effectiveness. Rifles such as the Austrian Lorenz are typical of those bought in Europe, while the British Enfield saw more usage than most home-built designs.

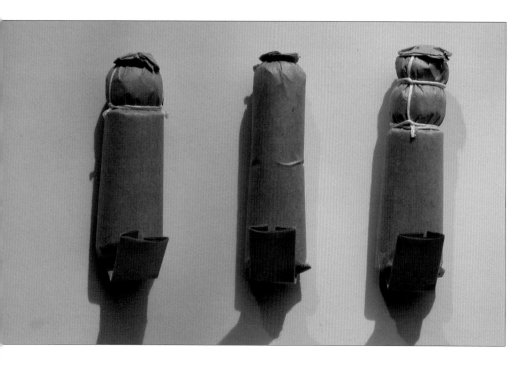

Civil War ammunition came in many different shapes and sizes but these three paper cartridges were among the most common. On the far left is the .69 caliber ball cartridge as used by many of the smooth-bore musket conversions that were in widespread use on both sides at the beginning of the war. In the middle is a .58 caliber ball cartridge as used by the Model 1861 Springfield or Enfield rifles, and on the right a .69 caliber buck and ball cartridge. The latter combined buckshot with a lead ball to create maximum damage.

At the outset of war many soldiers, particularly from the South, were poorly equipped. This Confederate private has brought his shotgun along, on the basis that what has served him well hunting jackrabbits for the pot, will work on larger targets.

A few poor soldiers of both sides went to war still equipped with old-fashioned flintlock smoothbore muzzleloading muskets, where, when the trigger was pulled, a piece of flint was hammered into a metal plate to produce a shower of sparks which ignited the main charge. Flintlock muskets had already been around for over 200 years, and were never particularly reliable, especially in rain or damp weather. Their smoothbore barrel made them extremely inaccurate, and the best that could be hoped for was that a large formation of infantry could perhaps score hits on another, equally large formation at ranges of less than 100 yards. The Model 1816, made at Harpers Ferry, Springfield, and elsewhere, is a typical example.

Most Civil War soldiers, however, carried rifled percussion arms. A tiny quantity of a compound known as "fulminates" was used as a primer, usually held in a small copper or brass cap, which would be fitted over a hollow nipple, with a tube leading to the breech. When the trigger was pulled, a spring-loaded hammer slammed down on the cap, igniting the primer, which itself ignited the main charge. It was a much more reliable system, and well able to operate in wet conditions.

Rifling, with spiral grooves in the lining of the barrel causing the projectile to spin, could dramatically increase range and accuracy. The problem for a muzzle-loader was that for accuracy you needed a bullet that fitted tightly into the barrel rifling. But such a tight fit made it difficult to ram the bullet down the barrel when loading, and almost impossible to do so once the barrel was fouled with the residue of a few shots. In the Civil War, most rifles used a conical expanding ball or "Minie" bullet with enough clearance to allow it to be easily loaded down the barrel, but with a thin skirt around its base, which was forced outward by the explosion of the gasses behind it, thus causing a gas seal and engaging with the rifling. The most popular of these rifles was the superb Springfield Model 1861, which became the nearest thing to a standard Civil War arm.

For most muzzle-loading rifles, projectile and powder came wrapped in a paper cartridge, and the same drill was used to load and fire, no matter what model of weapon the soldier had. Normally the infantryman would ground the butt of his rifle near his feet, then taking a paper cartridge from his pouch, tear off the end containing the bullet with his teeth, retaining the bullet within the cartridge. The powder would be poured down the barrel, then the bullet inserted in the muzzle, after which the soldier would draw his ramrod and ram the bullet down the barrel until it sat firmly on the powder below. The ramrod was stowed, then the rifle brought up until it was pointing slightly higher than level. The soldier would then withdraw a percussion cap from the relevant pouch and fix it to the nipple. On the command, the rifle would be brought to the shoulder and pointed in the general direction of the target and the hammer cocked. On the order "Fire," the soldier and his comrades would fire together in a massed volley.

It all sounds neat and easy, and in theory a trained soldier should have been able to fire up to three aimed shots a minute. But it was a very different story in the noise, smoke, confusion, and terror of battle, where fumbling fingers dropped percussion caps, where barrel-fouling slowed loading of the bullet, where ramrods would be left in the barrel, and where a man could see his comrades being killed and mutilated around him.

The luckier infantrymen had breechloading rifles or carbines using metallic cartridges, with the primer, powder and bullet held in a neat, consistent package. Breechloaders had been tried before, but it wasn't until the advent of the metallic cartridge that a reliable seal could be created. A man with a cartridge breechloader could feed a new round in and be ready to fire his next shot in a matter of seconds, and without having to shift his grip or aim. The luckiest of all had breechloading repeaters, such as the Spencer rifles and carbines, with multiple cartridges held in a magazine that allowed the firer to pump out a fearsome rate of fire, with little fear of misfire.

Handling large formations of men on the battlefield was a complex and difficult task, and in the early part of the war most regiments followed a drill manual published in 1860 by Lt. Col. William Hardee (later a Confederate General). A subsequent 1862 manual by Brigadier General Silas Casey simplified Hardee's drill and was also used by both sides. In essence, both manuals followed Napoleonic principles, where massed formations would march around the battlefield and blaze away at each other from close range.

While such tactics were adequate in the era of smoothbore muskets, they were a recipe for extremely high casualties in the face of much more devastating rifle fire and artillery of the Civil War. Attempts were made by many officers to modify them, and such innovations included the greater use of skirmishers, attempts to manuever in open-order formations or single lines, and "fire and movement" tactics. These only had limited success, and proved to be almost impossible to manage with the hastily trained troops that formed the bulk of both armies.

In the main, throughout the war, infantrymen had to stand shoulder to shoulder with their comrades, and face a storm of bullet and shell without dodging, taking cover, or running away. Even after 140 years, one can only wonder at their determination and admire their courage.

A severely understrength Company H of the 44th Indiana infantry line up, with their sword bayonets fitted to their Enfield rifles. The British Enfields were the most common foreign weapon to serve in the war.

Effective enough as a rifle, as a privately procured weapon which needed its own ammunition, this may not have been an ideal choice for general battlefield use.

Allen and Wheelock Drop Block Rifle

Ethan Allen (1806–1871) was a gunsmith operating in and around Worcester, Massachusetts and who

SPECIFICATIONS

Type: percussion rifle muskets

Origin: Bridesburg Machine Works,
    Philadelphia, Pennsylvania

Caliber: .58 and .64

Barrel Length: 40 in

Bridesburg Muskets

At the time of the outbreak of war, the Bridesburg Machine Works were well-established and successful manufacturers of cotton and wool milling machines. The owners, Alfred Jenks and his son Barton, made a quick – and very perceptive –

formed a number of companies through his working life. During the period he traded as "Allen and Wheelock" he produced this neat single shot breechloader from around 1860 to 1871. It uses a dropping breechblock, which moves down when the trigger guard is lowered, ejecting the case and allowing a fresh round to be inserted. Some saw military service in the Civil War as privately procured weapons.

SPECIFICATIONS

Type: single-shot breechloading rimfire rifle

Origin: Allen & Wheelock, Worcester, Massachusetts

Caliber: .42 A&W rimfire

Barrel Length: 26 in

business decision and built a huge new factory for arms production. By 1863, the factory housed some 150 workers who were producing approximately 5,000 U.S. government pattern muskets per month. By the time the factory closed at the end of the war it had manufactured just under 100,000 rifles for the Union government.

Above is a .64 caliber Model 1861 musket with a 40-inch barrel – the U.S. government eagle and the maker's name are just visible on the lock plate

The detail above shows that the percussion nipple is missing on this example.

This one is a Model 1863 .58 caliber musket with a 40-inch barrel.

The Brown Rifle was both ornate and highly functional.

The back-action lock and flamboyant brass furniture, combined with the massive barrel, made for a heavy and cumbersome rifle.

The patchbox lid opens ready to dispense a paper patch to seal the bullet in the bore.

SPECIFICATIONS

Type: percussion rifle

Origin: J. F. Brown, Haverhill, Massachusetts

Caliber: .45

Barrel Length: 32.5 in

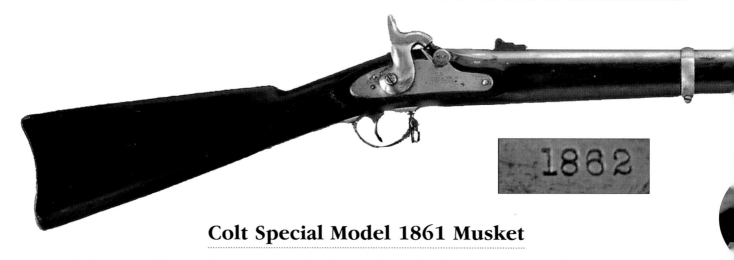

Colt Special Model 1861 Musket

In the late 1850s the British government placed an order with Robbins & Lawrence of Windsor, Vermont, for a large quantity of Enfield Pattern 1853 muskets to be made according to the "American system" of machine-made, totally interchangeable parts. Work had already started when the Crimean War broke out and the American company, anticipating even more orders, purchased more manufacturing machinery from Britain. At the same time, Colonel Colt was in London trying to persuade the government to place an order with him, telling them that if they ordered a million muskets he would supply them at half the price they were currently paying. When the Crimean War ended however, the British canceled their contracts with Robbins & Lawrence (who went bankrupt) and ended their discussions with Colt.

J.F. Brown Target/Sniper Rifle

This very interesting target shooter was also used as a sniper rifle during the Civil War, when it represented the very latest technology. The weapon was made by J.F. Brown, who was based in Poplin from 1840 to 1856 and Fremont from 1856 to 1859, both in New Hampshire, and in Haverhill, Massachusetts from 1859 until his death in 1904. The telescopic sight was manufactured by L.M. Amadon of Bellows Falls, Vermont, who was one of the pioneers of such devices. Both Amadon and Brown were famous in their time for the very high quality of their products.

During the Civil War, Union forces formed Sharpshooter units in which most of the men were armed with Sharp's rifles, but for long-range sniping a few were armed with the much heavier Brown rifle, of the type seen here. The massive cast-steel, octagonal barrel is 32.5 inches long and contributes the most to the overall weight of 30 pounds. The round section a the end of the barrel is a "false muzzle," which was designed to help load the conical-shaped "picket" bullets correctly without damaging the all-important rifling at the true muzzle; it was removed prior to firing. The paper patches used in loading were stored in the elaborately engraved patchbox. The sight could be adjusted by vertical and horizontal screws at the rear end, making it clear this rifle was intended for the highest degree of accuracy. The weight of the Brown rifle was such that the firer would have had to use a rest, but no fitting can be seen on this rifle.

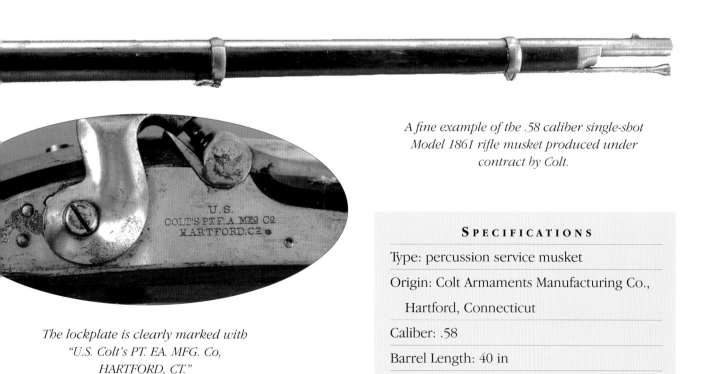

A fine example of the .58 caliber single-shot Model 1861 rifle musket produced under contract by Colt.

The lockplate is clearly marked with "U.S. Colt's PT. EA. MFG. Co, HARTFORD, CT."

SPECIFICATIONS

Type: percussion service musket

Origin: Colt Armaments Manufacturing Co., Hartford, Connecticut

Caliber: .58

Barrel Length: 40 in

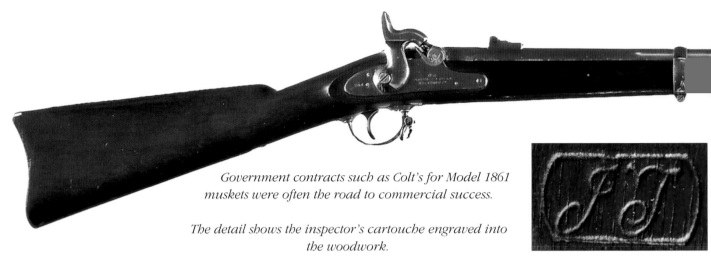

Government contracts such as Colt's for Model 1861 muskets were often the road to commercial success.

The detail shows the inspector's cartouche engraved into the woodwork.

Perhaps not the latest technology, but a ball from this converted smooth-bore would have had a devastating effect on its target – assuming it could hit it.

Deringer Model 1817 Percussion Conversion

Henry Deringer Sr. set up business in Philadelphia in the 1760s, and over time won various contracts to produce government pattern flintlock muskets and rifles. Deringer was one of the companies

Dickson Nelson & Co Rifle

Dickson, Nelson and Co. manufactured rifles for the Confederacy based on the flintlock Model 1814. This one appears to be a Model 1814 modified to percussion firing by the addition of the Dickson Nelson lockplate and nipple.

On the outbreak of the Civil War, Colt immediately offered to produce vast numbers of the "Colt Special" which, he claimed, combined the best features of the Springfield Model 1861 and the Enfield Pattern 1853. In reality it was a Model 1861 simply re-engineered in order to make it suitable for manufacture on the Enfield machinery that Colt had already bought from the bankrupt Robbins & Lawrence. Colt won his orders and deliveries started in September 1862, with production also being undertaken by Amoskeag, who made a total of 27,001 units, and Lamson, Goodnow & Yale (50,000), while Colt made some 131,000. The two examples shown (here and on the previous page) were made at the Colt factory at Hartford, Connecticut.

that won contracts to manufacture the Model 1817 Rifle musket, often known as the "Common Rifle." Many were later converted to percussion firing and saw service in the Civil War. The one shown was converted using the "Belgian" method, where a piece of brass was inserted into the lockplate where the priming pan and frizzen used to be, and a percussion nipple threaded into the barrel vent hole.

SPECIFICATIONS

Type: percussion modified rifle

Origin: Henry Deringer, Philadelphia,
    Pennsylvania

Caliber: .54

Barrel Length: 36 in

SPECIFICATIONS

Type: percussion modified rifle

Origin: Dickson Nelson & Co., Adairsville,
    Georgia and Dawson, Georgia

Caliber: .64

Barrel Length: 33.5 in

This Southern-manufactured smoothbore musket is complete with a brass patchbox. In most cases such frills were later dispensed with under the pressure of wartime production and need to conserve metal.

Well engineered and widely available the Enfield was a popular weapon with both sides. This one was made in England by Potts and Hunt.

This weapon carries CSA stampings, including the inventory mark "729" engraved into the brass buttplate.

Enfield Pattern 1853 Rifle Musket (3-band)

When the Civil War started both sides looked overseas to make up the shortfall in their infantry weapons. While a range of longarms was procured, the most popular foreign arm was the Enfield Pattern 1853, and it became one of the most common arms of the line in the war. One reason was that, while nominally in .577 caliber, it could also fire the .58 Springfield round, simplifying the supply of ammunition in the field.

The Enfield was originally developed for the British army, a decision forced on them by reports of the effectiveness of French Minie rifles. It fired an improved version of the Minie round, where the elongated bullet had no plug, but instead a hollow base, into which the expanding gasses blew, flaring out the edge of the bullet until it engaged with the rifling.

The Enfield was used by both sides in the war, but the majority were carried by soldiers of the Confederacy. When the war became a growing certainty the Chief of Ordnance of the Confederacy, Colonel Josiah Gorgas, was only too aware of the fact that manufacturing industry in the South could not supply enough arms to properly equip his forces. He sent his agent, Caleb Huse, to England and other European countries to buy arms. Because of the bad feeling over the War of Independence and that of 1812, and perhaps closer cultural affinities with the Southern States, England particularly wished to support the Confederate war effort. Huse managed to procure over 400,000 of the Pattern 1853 series, and it became the most predominant arm of the Confederate infantry.

SPECIFICATIONS

Type: muzzle-loading percussion rifle

Origin: Various

Caliber: .577

Barrel Length: 39 in

The uniforms may be non-regulation, but the Enfield rifles, socket bayonets and determined attitude make this small group a force to be reckoned with.

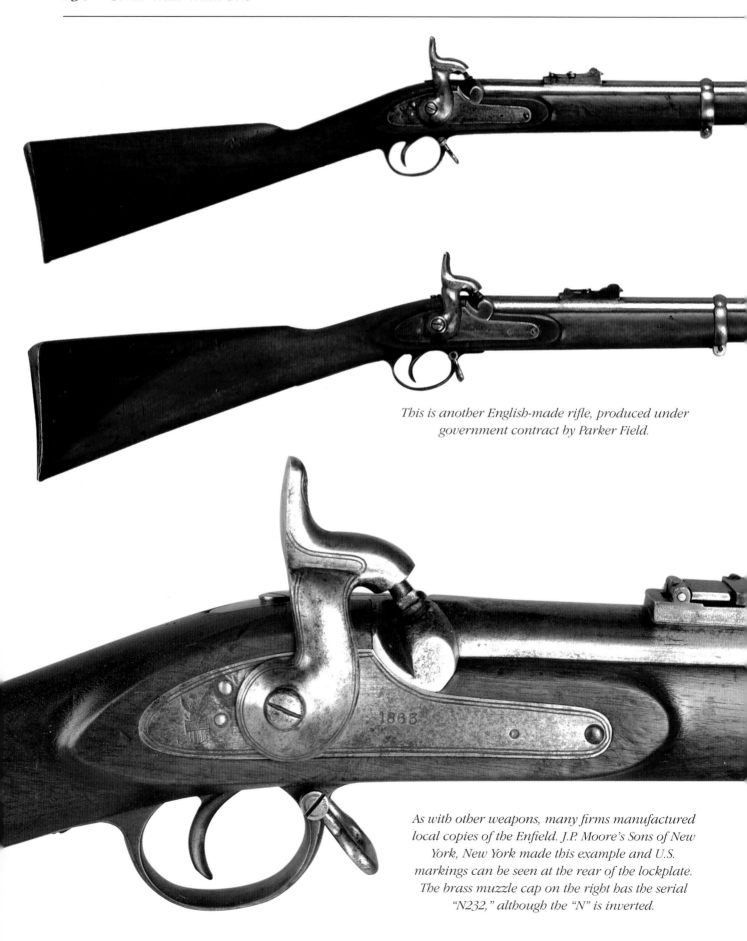

This is another English-made rifle, produced under government contract by Parker Field.

As with other weapons, many firms manufactured local copies of the Enfield. J.P. Moore's Sons of New York, New York made this example and U.S. markings can be seen at the rear of the lockplate. The brass muzzle cap on the right has the serial "N232," although the "N" is inverted.

The rifle above was made in England by Barnett and saw service in the Civil War. Relatively light, well made, popular and effective, the Enfield was the first British weapon to use metal bands to fix the barrel to the stock. The standard infantry rifle with the 39-inch barrel used three such bands, hence the "3-Band" designation.

The Union used the Enfield too, and this close-up shows New Jersey surcharge markings on the barrel and stock. Most Model 1853s were made at the Royal Ordnance Factory in Enfield, London, while various contractors, usually using the markings of the Tower Armouries, England made others.

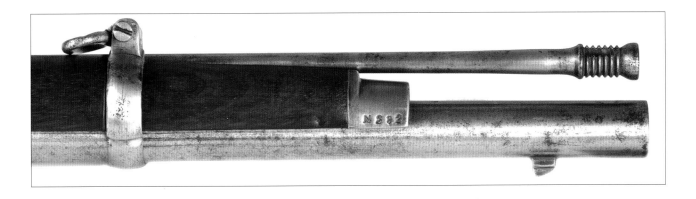

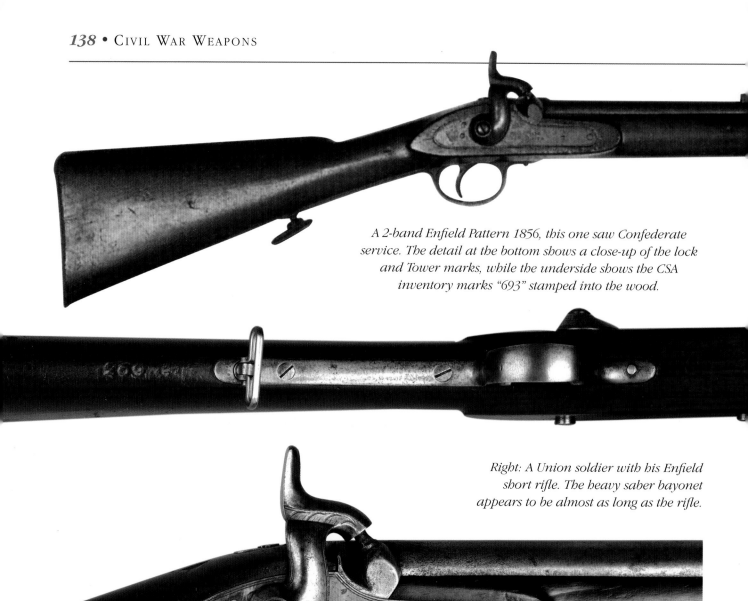

A 2-band Enfield Pattern 1856, this one saw Confederate service. The detail at the bottom shows a close-up of the lock and Tower marks, while the underside shows the CSA inventory marks "693" stamped into the wood.

Right: A Union soldier with his Enfield short rifle. The heavy saber bayonet appears to be almost as long as the rifle.

Enfield Pattern 1856 Rifle Musket (2-band)

SPECIFICATIONS

Type: muzzle-loading percussion rifle

Origin: Enfield, England and Tower
    Armouries, England

Caliber: .577

Barrel Length: 33 in

The Enfield rifle, while effective, was also a long piece, and could be cumbersome to aim quickly. A shorter version was produced, with the barrel reduced by 6 inches, and can be identified by the fact it has only two metal bands securing the barrel to the stock. In British service it was issued to rifleman skirmishers and to sergeants in line regiments. Many were procured for service in the Civil War.

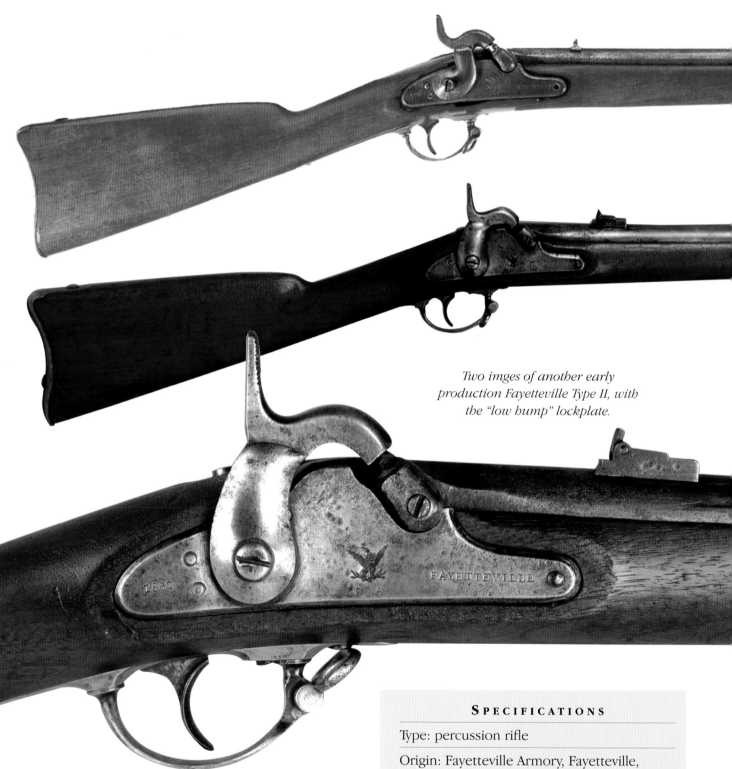

Two imges of another early production Fayetteville Type II, with the "low bump" lockplate.

A close-up of the lock reveals the American eagle and Fayetteville stamps. Both are reasonably well preserved.

SPECIFICATIONS

Type: percussion rifle

Origin: Fayetteville Armory, Fayetteville, North Carolina

Caliber: .58

Barrel Length: 33 in

Shown above is a Fayetteville Type II with the "low hump" lockplate. The earlier Type I had a lock plate with a higher hump to the same profile as the Maynard Tape Primer system, although the Maynard system was never fitted. This Type II shows the results of over-enthusiastic cleaning and sanding at some point in its history.

Fayetteville Confederate Rifle

One of the most daring operations of the Civil War was the Confederate raid on the Harper's Ferry Armory in April 1861, during which the raiders removed parts and gunmaking equipment before destroying this vital government production facility. Captured components, tools and equipment were removed to enable production to take place at the Confederate armories at Richmond and Fayetteville.

Most of the production at Fayetteville was based on the design of the Model 1855 percussion rifle, and two examples are shown here. The original Model 1855 used the Maynard Tape Primer system, and the captured tooling had been set up to produce lockplates to fit. The Confederate armories didn't use the Maynard system, but rather than redesign the tooling they carried on manufacturing lockplates to the same shape. Hence all Fayetteville (and Richmond) rifles have a distinctive "hump" in the lockplate that actually has no function.

The detail shows the brass buttplate with "CSA" stamp.

Greene Bolt-action Rifle

A good example of how the Civil War spanned developments in weapons technology. While some soldiers used conversions of smoothbore flintlock muskets, others had weapons such as is this very modern rifled breechloader. The first bolt-action rifle purchased by the U.S. government, some 900 were delivered during the War in March 1863. Patented by Lt. Col. J. Durrell Greene, it used a twisted oval section bore similar to that developed by Charles Lancaster in England. The bullet fitted into the oval section, and the twist imparted a spin in the same way as rifling. The Greene was also unusual in that the hammer was underneath, in front of the trigger guard. After locking the bolt, the firer still had to insert a percussion priming cap on the nipple beneath the stock.

The breechloading concept of the Hall may have been futuristic for the times but its antiquated stock profile and furniture give its true age away.

SPECIFICATIONS

Type: breechloading, percussion rifle

Origin: Harper's Ferry Armory, Harper's Ferry, Virginia

Caliber: .52

Barrel Length: 32.6 in

SPECIFICATIONS

Type: single shot, bolt-action percussion rifle

Origin: A. H. Waters Armory, Millbury,
    Massachusetts

Caliber: .53

Barrel Length: 35 in

Hall Model 1841 Rifle

John Hancock Hall (1778–1841) was a gun designer who hailed from North Yarmouth, Maine. In 1811, he was a joint patentee with William Thornton of Washington, D.C., of a novel breechloading flintlock rifle with a tip-up breech chamber, in which the breech lock and chamber were incorporated into a single unit. This was manufactured and sold at Portland, Maine from 1811 to 1816, but Hall then moved to Harper's Ferry, Virginia and his weapon was adopted as an official U.S. Army rifle in 1819, the first breechloader to be so standardized. Hall designed the machinery for his weapon's production, which was housed in a separate building (known for many years as "the rifle works," and remained there until 1840, supervising the manufacture of weapons to his patent.

The Model 1841 is effectively the percussion version of the Hall Model 1819, and thousands served in the Civil War. The one shown here is an early transition model, and apart from the lock and modified rifling, is almost identical to the Model 1819. Later production had a different breech release catch in front of the trigger guard.

Above: Dated 1838, this one is a Type III with "bright" steelwork. The frizzen (metal plate) is open, exposing the pan where the small priming charge of powder would be placed.

A Model 1816 after conversion to percussion fire. The barrel has also been rifled, and sights fitted.

Above: This Type I is dated 1820, has a browned barrel and the separate sling swivel lug. The open jaws of the hammer show where a piece of flint would have been clamped.

Above: The integral trigger guard and browned metal work can be seen on this Type II. The position of the flint and frizzen demonstrates how the impact of flint on metal would cause a shower of sparks to ignite the primer charge.

Harper's Ferry Model 1816 Musket

Harper's Ferry is named after Robert Harper, an English immigrant, who established a watermill there in 1748. It was personally selected by George Washington as the site for a national gun foundry and it was authorized by Congress in 1794, with production starting in 1795. At this time, 40 workers produced 245 flintlocks muskets monthly.

The Harper's Ferry Model 1816 was manufactured from 1817 to 1844 with three minor variations. The original, known as the Type I, which was produced from 1817 to 1821, had the lower sling swivel attached to a separate lug forward of the trigger guard. The Type II (1821 onwards) had the rear sling swivel incorporated into the trigger guard. Until 1832, both Type I and the Type II were produced with a "browned" barrel to reduce rusting, but in 1832 this was discontinued. From then on barrels were "bright" until production ended in 1844, and it's this production that is identified as the Type III. In the 1850s many were altered to percussion firing and some of these were altered yet again during the Civil War, with rifled barrels, sights and a "patent breech."

SPECIFICATIONS

Type: muzzle-loading, flintlock musket

Origin: Harper's Ferry Armory, Harper's
    Ferry, Virginia,

Caliber: .69

Barrel Length: 42 in

Harper's Ferry Model 1841 "Mississippi Rifle"

When production of the Hall breechloading rifle ended in 1841, the Harper's Ferry "rifle works" was converted to manufacture the newly-adopted U.S. Model 1841 rifle. Some 25,000 were produced at Harper's Ferry between 1846 and 1855. The Model 1841 will always be known as the "Mississippi rifle" in memory of the troops who used it during the Mexican-American War, particularly at the Battle of Buena Vista against General Santa Anna's Mexican army in February 1847.

In that battle, Colonel Jefferson Davis's 1st Mississippi Rifles, armed with the new muzzle-loading "U.S. Model 1841 Percussion Rifle," turned the tide for the heavily outnumbered U.S. troops, and this weapon has been known ever since been known as the "Mississippi rifle" in their honor.

SPECIFICATIONS

Type: muzzle-loading, percussion rifle

Origin: Harper's Ferry Armory, Harper's Ferry, Virginia

Caliber: .54

Barrel Length: 33 in

*Above: This example is dated 1850 and appears to be in original
condition and is complete except for the sling swivels.*

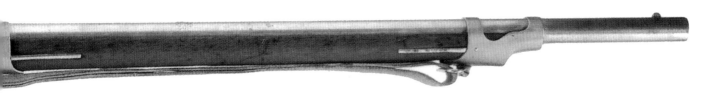

*Above: Another Model 1841, though not in as complete condition. The small
chain holds a protective cap that fits over the nipple when not in action.*

*The rifle above has the original rearsight and bayonet mount. The
detail below shows the opened patchbox, complete with spare nipple,
balls and patch material.*

Harper's Ferry Model 1842 Musket

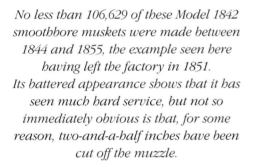

No less than 106,629 of these Model 1842 smoothbore muskets were made between 1844 and 1855, the example seen here having left the factory in 1851.
Its battered appearance shows that it has seen much hard service, but not so immediately obvious is that, for some reason, two-and-a-half inches have been cut off the muzzle.

SPECIFICATIONS

Type: muzzle-loading, percussion
   musket

Origin: Harper's Ferry Armory,
   Harper's Ferry, Virginia

Caliber: .69

Barrel Length: 42 in

This soldier is in the studio fully kitted out with uniform, musket, belts, backpack and pouches, all clean and in good condition. A few months on campaign and he will look a very different person.

Far Right: Lt. Parker and two men from the 4th Michigan pose with musket, bayonet, sword and revolver – the tools of the infantryman. The man crouching on the left was probably a "contraband," an escaped slave, but now most likely acting as a manservant to Parker.

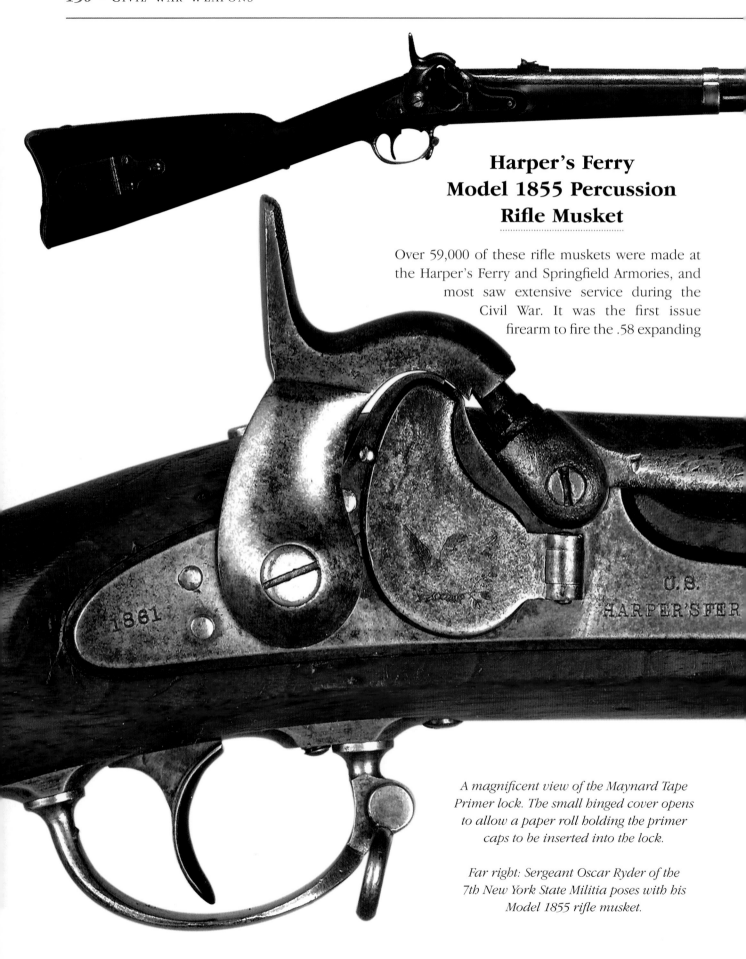

Harper's Ferry Model 1855 Percussion Rifle Musket

Over 59,000 of these rifle muskets were made at the Harper's Ferry and Springfield Armories, and most saw extensive service during the Civil War. It was the first issue firearm to fire the .58 expanding

A magnificent view of the Maynard Tape Primer lock. The small hinged cover opens to allow a paper roll holding the primer caps to be inserted into the lock.

Far right: Sergeant Oscar Ryder of the 7th New York State Militia poses with his Model 1855 rifle musket.

Minie bullet, and also used the Maynard Tape Priming system instead of individual percussion primer caps. This example is dated 1861, which means that it is quite rare, as the Harper's Ferry Armory stopped production after being destroyed by Confederate forces in the April of that year. Captured Model 1855 tooling and components were used by the Confederates to make Fayetteville and Richmond muskets.

SPECIFICATIONS

Type: muzzle-loading, percussion musket

Origin: Harper's Ferry Armory, Harper's
    Ferry, Virginia

Caliber: .58

Barrel Length: 40 in

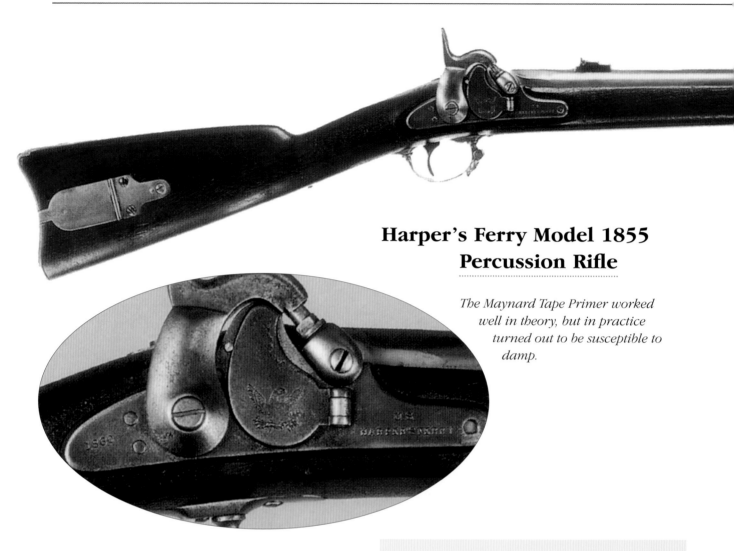

Harper's Ferry Model 1855 Percussion Rifle

The Maynard Tape Primer worked well in theory, but in practice turned out to be susceptible to damp.

A development of the Model 1855 rifle musket, the Model 1855 Rifle had a shorter barrel (at 33 inches) fixed to the stock by only two bands instead of three. It kept the same Maynard primer mechanism and used the same .58 Minie bullet. Only 7,613 of these rifles were made before the Armory was destroyed in 1861.

SPECIFICATIONS

Type: muzzle-loading, percussion rifle

Origin: Harper's Ferry Armory, Harper's Ferry, Virginia

Caliber: .58

Barrel Length: 33 in

A pair of well-equipped Union soldiers with Harper's Ferry rifles and sword bayonets.

A Model 1855 Rifle with brass patchbox and complete with brass-handled sabre bayonet. The Model 1855 was the last muzzle-loading rifle to be adopted by a significant national armory.

Henry Rifle

Invented and patented by B. Tyler Henry (1821–1898), the Model 1860 was chambered for the .44 Henry cartridge, and had a 15-round, tubular magazine under the barrel. It had an octagonal 24-inch barrel with no foregrip, but with a walnut buttstock and a brass buttplate. Some 14,000 of these rifles were made between 1861 and 1866, of which the early examples had iron frames and the remainder, as seen here, brass frame. When the ring trigger was pushed forward the rearmost round in the magazine was forced in to a scoop-shaped carrier by the magazine spring. The hammer was then cocked and the ring trigger drawn to the rear, which lifted the round into the chamber.

The Henry rifle represented some significant advances, the most important being that the fifteen-round magazine gave the shooter a major increase in firepower. It also, however, suffered from some

This particular weapon, with serial number 8794, has been identified as one of a batch of Henrys issued to troops on guard duties in the area of Washington D.C., in the latter part of the Civil War.

SPECIFICATIONS

Type: tubular-magazine, lever-action rifle

Origin: New Haven Arms Co., New Haven, Connecticut

Caliber: .44 Henry

Barrel Length: 24.25 in

Overleaf: Company A, 7th Illinois Color Guard, were tasked with defending Washington from Confederate attack. They were equipped with the fast-firing Henry rifle.

drawbacks, several of which had tactical implications. The first was that the shooter's forehand held the barrel, which became very hot in a prolonged engagement. The second, and more important, was that the tubular magazine had to be disengaged and reloaded from the front, which meant that the weapon had to be taken out of action and engage the shooter's attention until the task had been completed. Thirdly, the magazine had slots, which allowed dirt to enter.

The company changed its name from the New Haven Arms Company to the Henry Repeating Rifle Company in 1865 and to the Winchester Repeating Arms Company in 1866. This meant that when these problems were overcome in a new model that was introduced that year, it carried the now legendary name of the "Winchester Model 1866."

Another brass frame Henry, the rifle below carries the serial number 788. The detail shows how a previous owner has fitted his own rearsight into a slot cut into the barrel, and which has been made from an "Indian head" penny.

Justice Rifle Musket

P.S. Justice began manufacturing rifles and rifle muskets as the Civil War broke out in 1861, one of many new manufacturers trying to meet the rapid demand for weapons from Union forces. Justice rifles were not of

The Leonard Rifle closely resembled the Brown Rifle – and both had their origins in New England.

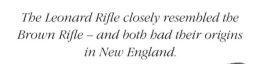

Leonard Percussion Target Rifle

Artemis Leonard and his son produced weapons from 1840 to 1860 in Saxtons River, Vermont. This superbly made precision weapon has a remarkably heavy octagonal barrel and tubular telescopic sight. Fine engraving decorates the lock and hammer, while the stock has engraved checkering. The lock is the rear action type, with the springs and lockplate behind the hammer. An accurate weapon such as this is typical of the private purchases that found use as sniper rifles during the Civil War.

SPECIFICATIONS

Type: percussion target rifle with telescopic

sight

Origin: Leonard & Son, Saxtons River,

Vermont

Caliber: .48

Barrel Length: 31 in

particularly high quality, but they were effective enough and were some of the first wartime production to get into the hands of the fighting men. Most were assembled from a mixture of existing components, and this 1861 rifle has some parts dated 1829. It also has the ramrod and one barrel restraining band missing.

SPECIFICATIONS
Type: percussion rifle musket
Origin: P. S. Justice, Philadelphia, Pennsylvania
Caliber: .69
Barrel Length: 39 in

Left: The scrollwork engraving on the underside of the trigger guard shows careful craftsmanship.

The rear action lock is beautifully engineered and the stock has fine checkering to improve grip.

Lindsay Two-shot Musket

There were many attempts to find a means of delivering more than one shot from the same weapon without reloading, which led eventually to revolvers and cartridge-firing self-loading and automatic weapons. It was, however, a long search and numerous inventors in many countries produced some real curiosities along the way. John Parker Lindsay of New York City, New York was one of those who devoted much effort to solving this problem and patented a system in which two

SPECIFICATIONS

Type: rifled percussion musket

Origin: Austro-Hungarian state arsenals

Caliber: .54 or .58

Barrel Length: 40 in

Lorenz Model 1854 Rifle Musket

This weapon was designed by Lieutenant Joseph Lorenz of the Imperial Austro-Hungarian Army and entered service with the army in 1854. When the Civil War broke out purchasers from both the Union and the Confederacy scoured Europe looking for firearms of any sort, and as the Lorenz

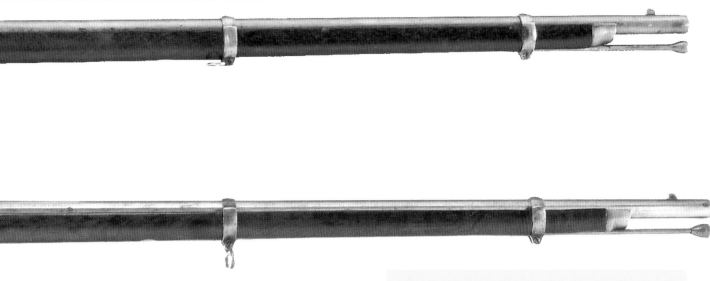

chambers fed into a single barrel, with the two shots being fired consecutively. He received a government order on December 17, 1863 for 1,000 muskets of this design, one of which is shown here. Lindsay muskets saw some service but the design turned out to be impractical for widespread military use. Unless it was loaded very carefully, it tended to fire both rounds at once, causing extreme recoil forces and endangering the user.

SPECIFICATIONS

Type: two-shot, single-barrel musket

Origin: J.P. Lindsay Manufacturing Company, New Haven, Connecticut

Caliber: .58

Barrel Length: 41 in

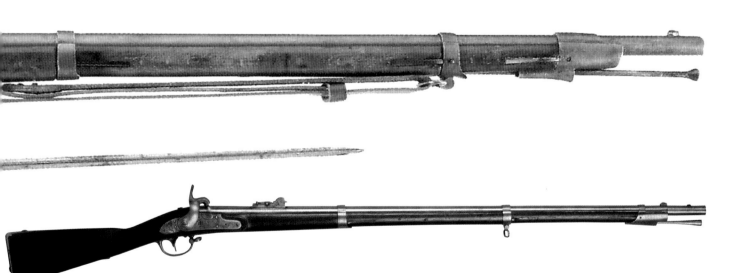

was being replaced by the Model 1862 rifle in Austro-Hungarian service, many thousands were readily available. As a result, the Model 1854 Lorenz rifled musket was widely used by both sides; the Union bought some 225,000 and the Confederacy approximately 100,000.

There were a number of variations among these imported weapons. Some were .54 caliber, others .58, and there were also different types of sight. The weapon was well-liked and was considered as accurate as the more widely used Enfield, although it tended to suffer from fouling. The top weapon seen here is .54 caliber with walnut stock and is in generally good condition. The lower is in .58 caliber.

The shape of the lock plate shows how the gun has been converted from flintlock with the outline of the ground off pan clearly visible.

SPECIFICATIONS

Type: muzzle-loading percussion musket

Origin: Royal Small Arms Factory, Enfield, England

Caliber: .75

Barrel Length: 39 in

A long stock and heavy barrel characterizes these
flintlock musket conversions.

Lovell Pattern 1839 Musket Conversion

George Lovell worked at the Royal Small Arms Factory in Enfield, England and developed this percussion conversion for obsolete British flintlock "Brown Bess" muskets in 1839. The conversion was never a particularly popular weapon, and was quickly superseded by the Enfield Rifle. The Civil War was a good opportunity for the British government to offload some obsolete stock, however, and many of these conversions ended up in the hands of Confederate soldiers.

This Lovell conversion musket saw service in the Civil War, and has
"LCB" carved into the stock.

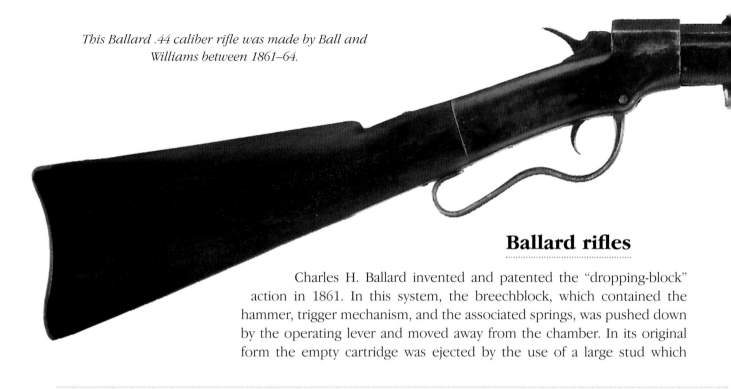

This Ballard .44 caliber rifle was made by Ball and Williams between 1861–64.

Ballard rifles

Charles H. Ballard invented and patented the "dropping-block" action in 1861. In this system, the breechblock, which contained the hammer, trigger mechanism, and the associated springs, was pushed down by the operating lever and moved away from the chamber. In its original form the empty cartridge was ejected by the use of a large stud which

Miller Parker's Snow Rifle

Parker's Snow were one of the manufacturers of the Model 1861 rifle musket, and this weapon was originally made for one of their Civil War contracts. From 1865 onwards, some 2,000 of the Parker's Snow rifles were subsequently converted to the patented breechloading system developed by William and George Miller (see above). By releasing a catch on top of the barrel, the breech assembly could be hinged upwards to allow a new round to be loaded. The Miller conversion fired a .58 centerfire metallic cartridge.

SPECIFICATIONS

Type: Type: percussion conversion rifle

Origin: Parker's Snow and Co., Meriden, Connecticutt

Caliber: .58 centerfire

Barrel Length: 31.5 in

projected below the fore-end, but from 1873 onwards, an extractor was activated by the operating lever. Ballard's patented rifles were manufactured by a variety of gunsmiths, including Ball & Williams (1861–4), R. Ball & Co. (1864–6), Merrimack Arms & Manufacturing (1867–9), and Brown Manufacturing (1869–73). We show a Civil War Ballard .44 caliber rifle, made by Ball & Williams, showing the combined operating lever/trigger guard and the stud beneath the forestock which controlled the extractor.

SPECIFICATIONS

Type: Ballard-patent rifle

Origin: Ball & Williams, Worcester, Massachusetts

Caliber: .44

Barrel Length: 22 in

Made in Meriden, Connecticut and proud of it!

Peabody Rifle

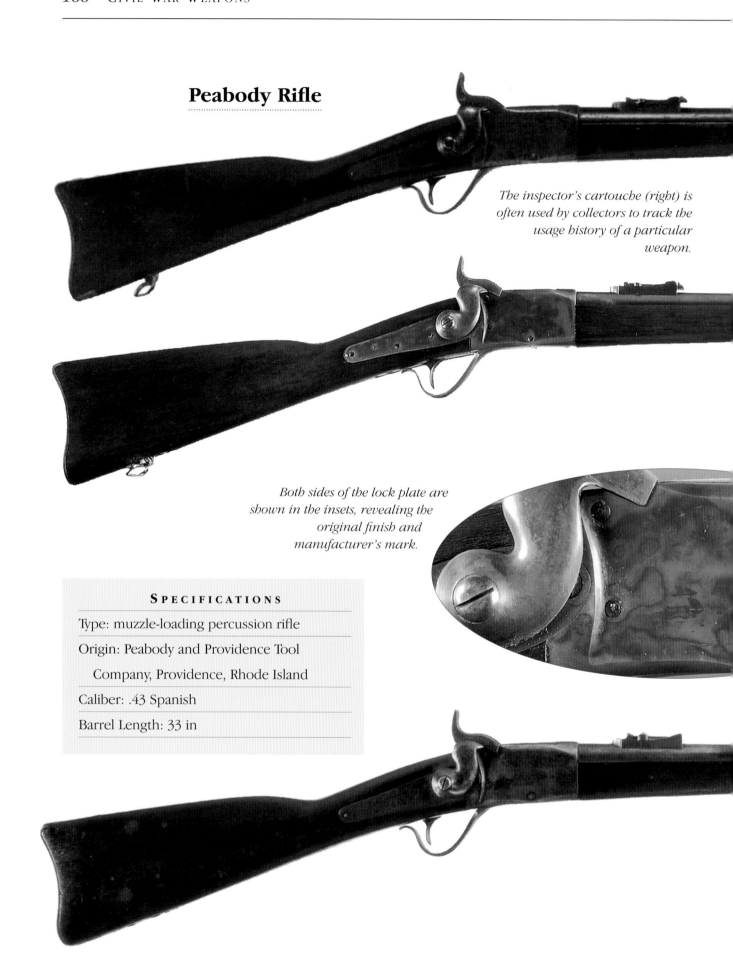

The inspector's cartouche (right) is often used by collectors to track the usage history of a particular weapon.

Both sides of the lock plate are shown in the insets, revealing the original finish and manufacturer's mark.

SPECIFICATIONS

Type: muzzle-loading percussion rifle

Origin: Peabody and Providence Tool
    Company, Providence, Rhode Island

Caliber: .43 Spanish

Barrel Length: 33 in

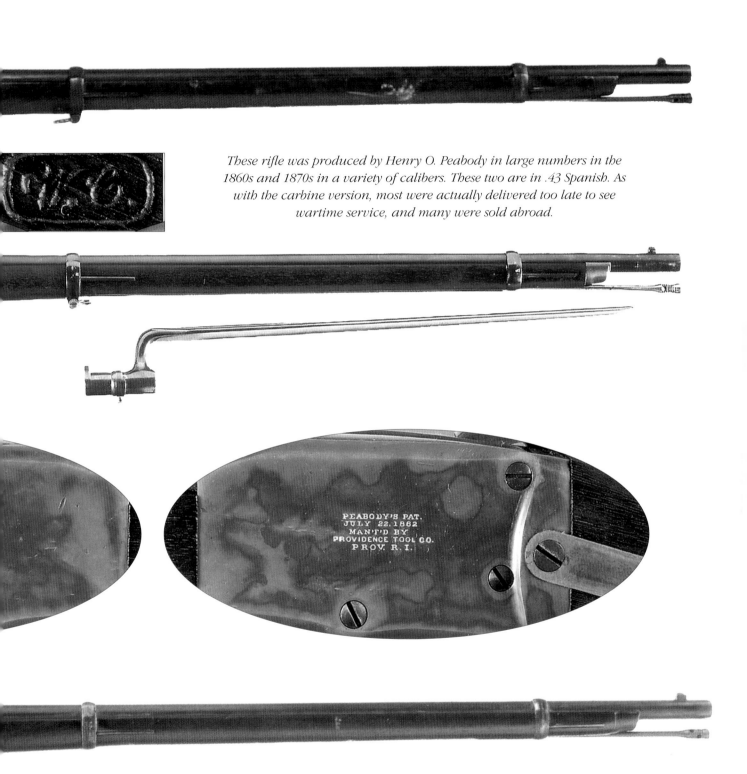

These rifle was produced by Henry O. Peabody in large numbers in the 1860s and 1870s in a variety of calibers. These two are in .43 Spanish. As with the carbine version, most were actually delivered too late to see wartime service, and many were sold abroad.

PEABODY'S PAT.
JULY 22.1862
MAN'F'D BY
PROVIDENCE TOOL CO.
PROV. R.I.

This example is in .45 caliber.

Pomeroy Muskets

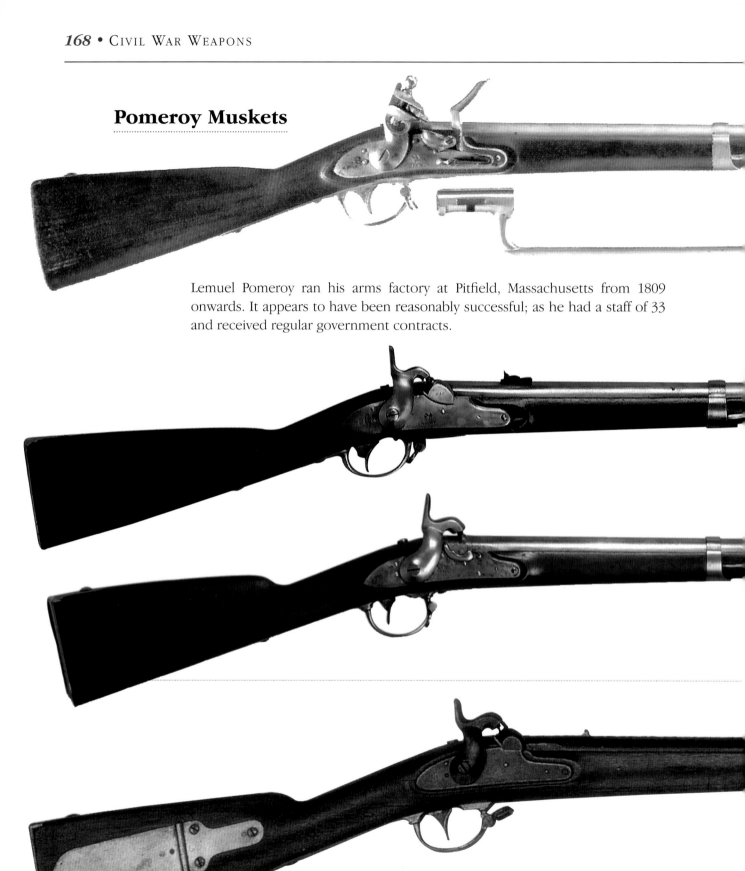

Lemuel Pomeroy ran his arms factory at Pitfield, Massachusetts from 1809 onwards. It appears to have been reasonably successful; as he had a staff of 33 and received regular government contracts.

One of the prettiest and most collectable guns of the Civil War.

The weapon seen here is a Pomeroy U.S. Model 1816 musket and bayonet produced in response to a contract for 5,000 such weapons.

SPECIFICATIONS

Type: breechloading musket

Origin: L. Pomeroy, Pitfield, Massachusetts

Caliber: .69

Barrel Length: 42 in

This image shows a Civil War-era Pomeroy after a "bolster" conversion to enable percussion fire, the conversion being carried out by Hewes and Phillips, of Newark, New Jersey.

Pomeroy also manufactured some 6,000 Model 1840 muskets such as the one shown here.

Remington Model 1841 Mississippi Rifle

Eliphalet Remington had a small forge business in Ilion, New York, and from around 1820 his son, Eliphalet Remington II, began making gun barrels there. Young Eli also tried to interest the U.S. government to make use of Remington barrels, made using their 'cast steel' process. By 1828 he was running the company, but at that point had no capacity for mass-producing complete weapons.

This was to change in 1845, when Eli II pulled off a couple of farsighted business deals to give the family firm a jump-start into the gunmaking business.

N.P. Ames of Chicopee Falls, Massachusetts were renowned sword makers and producers of superior gunmaking equipment and tools. They had contracts to produce the "Mule Ear" carbine for William Jenks, but in 1845 Remington offered to buy from Ames one of their contracts for 1,000 rifles. The deal also included the tooling and equipment which was shipped to Remington.

SPECIFICATIONS

Type: muzzleloading percussion musket

Origin: E. Remington and Sons, Ilion, New
   York

Caliber: .69

Barrel Length: 42 in

At around the same time, Remington also negotiated the purchase of a contract for 5,000 Model 1841 Mississippi Rifles held by John Griffiths of Cincinnati, Ohio. This deal also included machinery, although it's not clear if this was actually supplied. Remington delivered the first batch of Model 1841s in 1850, and used this success to gain subsequent government contracts for these and other military weapons. One of the giants of American gunmaking was now in business.

Remington M1816 Maynard Conversion

SPECIFICATIONS

Type: muzzle-loading, flintlock musket

Origin: see text

Caliber: .69

Barrel Length: 42 in

The Maynard Tape Priming system was fitted to many percussion muskets, including the Model 1816. This is one of a batch of about 20,000 that had new Maynard-type locks supplied by Remington, who bid for the contract in an attempt to keep their skilled gunmakers in work. The actual conversions were carried out from 1856–58 by the Frankford Arsenal, Philadelphia, Pennsylvania who also rifled the smoothbore barrels. Most saw military service in the Civil War.

An example of how obsolete weapons were kept in service by rifling them and converting them from flintlock to percussion, in this case using the Maynard Tape Primer system.

Opposite page: Don Troiani's painting of Company K, the Irish Zouaves, 69th New York State Militia, armed with Remingtons. As with all his paintings, the weapons and equipment are exact in every detail, and here the Tape Primer locks can be clearly seen.

Remington Model 1863 "Zouave" Rifle

Remington were awarded the contract to produce some 12,000 of this well made percussion rifle. Similar to the standard Model 1863, it was slightly shorter and had only two barrel bands. It's not known with any certainty why the name "Zouave" was given to this weapon, as there are no records to suggest it was issued particularly to these regiments with their unusual colorful clothing. As can be seen from the examples we show, many surviving Zouave rifles are in excellent condition, and it appears that many didn't see hard active service.

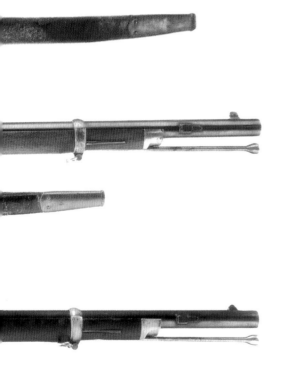

Several fine examples of this handsome weapon, complete with saber bayonets.

SPECIFICATIONS	
Type: muzzle-loading, percussion rifle	
Origin: E. Remington and Sons, Ilion, New York	
Caliber: .58	
Barrel Length: 33 in	

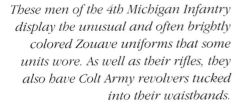

These men of the 4th Michigan Infantry display the unusual and often brightly colored Zouave uniforms that some units wore. As well as their rifles, they also have Colt Army revolvers tucked into their waistbands.

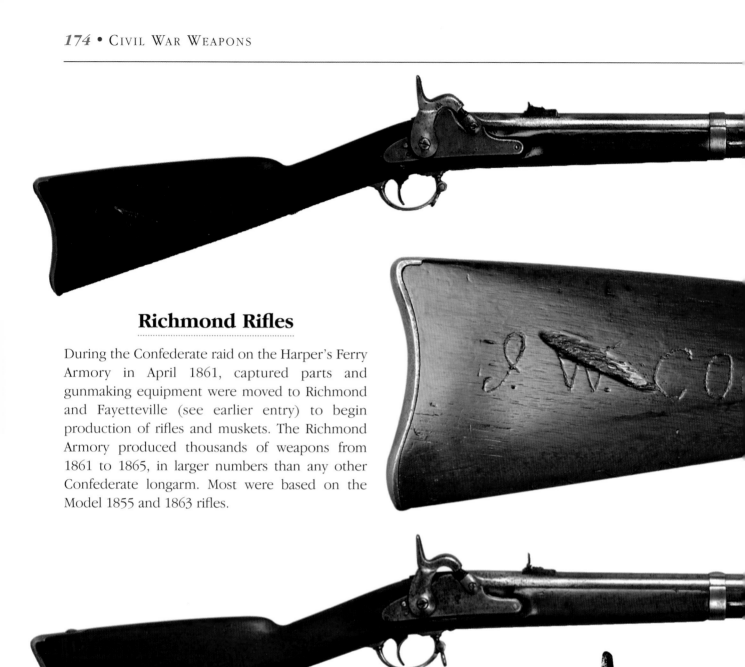

Richmond Rifles

During the Confederate raid on the Harper's Ferry Armory in April 1861, captured parts and gunmaking equipment were moved to Richmond and Fayetteville (see earlier entry) to begin production of rifles and muskets. The Richmond Armory produced thousands of weapons from 1861 to 1865, in larger numbers than any other Confederate longarm. Most were based on the Model 1855 and 1863 rifles.

SPECIFICATIONS
Type: percussion rifle
Origin: Richmond Armory, Richmond, Virginia
Caliber: .58
Barrel Length: 40 in

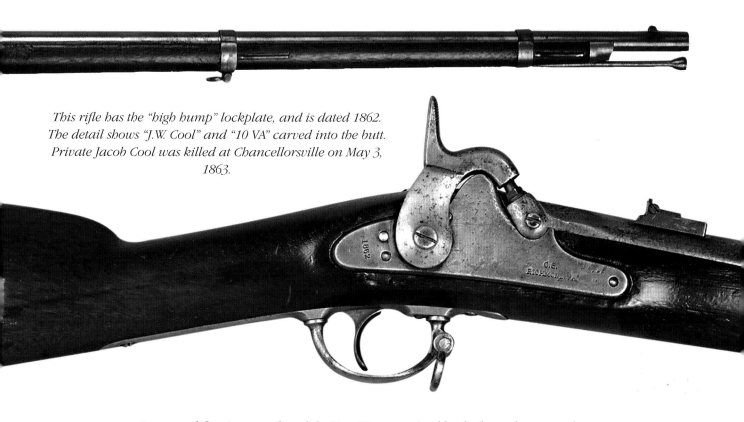

This rifle has the "high hump" lockplate, and is dated 1862. The detail shows "J.W. Cool" and "10 VA" carved into the butt. Private Jacob Cool was killed at Chancellorsville on May 3, 1863.

Later modifications produced the Type III, recognized by the lower hump on the lockplate. The one shown below is dated 1862, and the butt is carved with "James Clay 18 Virginia" and an array of 13 stars.

James Clay is known to have served in Company G of the 18th Virginia and participated in "Pickett's Charge" at Gettysburg.

Confederate production didn't use the Maynard system, but as the captured lockplate dies were set for the Model 1855 and its Maynard Tape primer lock, early Richmond lockplates followed the same shape. This gave an unusually high hump where the primer system would have been. Rifles to this design are usually referred to as Type I and Type II, and many minor variations exist. The one shown above is a Type II.

Don Troiani's "The Gray Wall" shows Confederate troops defending the road to Atlanta during the 1864 campaign. They are using a mixture of weapons including Cooks Bros and Enfield Rifle Muskets.

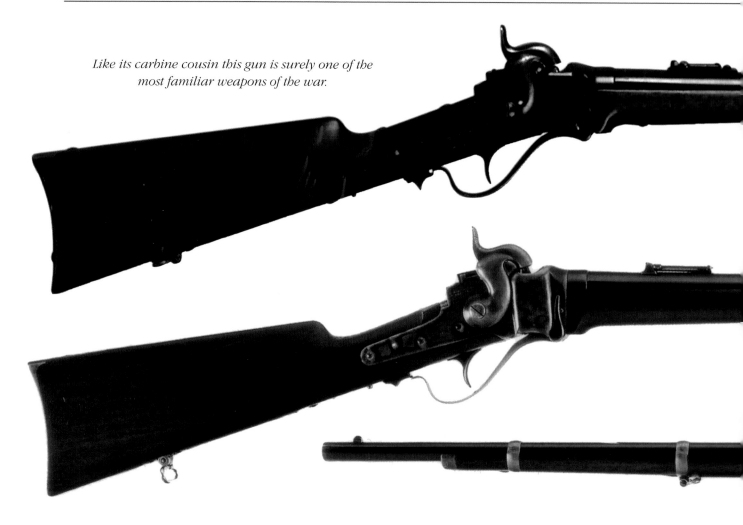

Like its carbine cousin this gun is surely one of the most familiar weapons of the war.

Sharps New Model Rifles

Christian Sharps was one of the most influential weapons designers of the time, making his name with a range of single-shot breechloading rifles and carbines. From around 1852 his early models were made by Robbins and Lawrence, in Windsor, Vermont, while Sharps marketed them from the Sharps Rifle Manufacturing Company, in Hartford, Connecticut.

A later redesign created the Sharps "New Model" weapons, recognizable from earlier models by the "straight breech" on the side of the frame (earlier ones had a definite slant). Although by this time Christian Sharps had severed all association with the company, and by 1854 had formed a new partnership with William Hankins (see the carbines chapter).

Both rifles and carbines used a paper or linen cartridge ignited by the Sharps patented integral pellet priming system. All types saw extensive service in the Civil War, and were sought after as extremely accurate and reliable breechloaders, able to put out a reasonably rapid rate of fire. The Model 1859 rifle shown here has the new style breech and is of a similar type to those used by Col. Hiram Berdan's 1st and 2nd regiments of U.S. Sharpshooters.

SPECIFICATIONS

Type: single-shot, breechloading percussion rifle

Origin: Sharps Rifle Manufacturing Company, Hartford, Connecticut

Caliber: .52

Barrel Length: 30 in

This gun was very accurate hence its use by Sharpshooting units.

*Two views of a fine Model 1865; one that was supplied
as a sales sample to the French government.*

*Detail of the reverse side of the distinctive
upright breech molding.*

This is one of a very small batch made for a U.S. Army trial immediately following the Civil War. It is chambered for the .46 round and has a 31-inch barrel; it is fitted with both the Stabler magazine cut-off and the external Spencer cut-off.

SPECIFICATIONS

Type: magazine-fed repeating rifle	
Origin: Spencer Repeating Rifle Co., Boston, Massachusetts	
Caliber: .56-56	
Barrel Length: 30 in	

The brass studs on the stock of the gun above probably indicate Native American ownership at some time after the war. These rifles were so effective that they remained in service throughout the Frontier period.

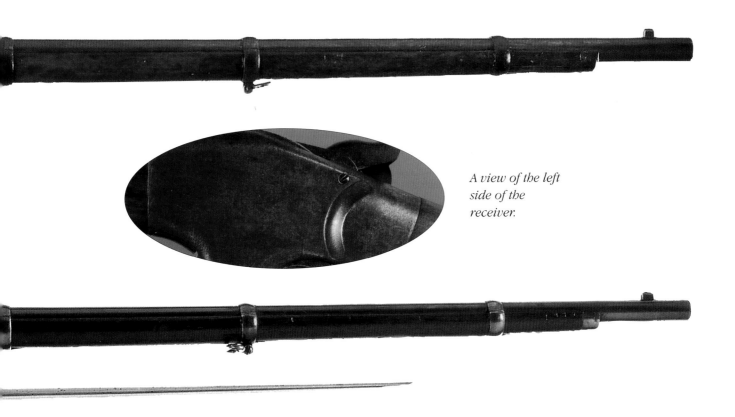

A view of the left side of the receiver.

Spencer Model 1860 Rifle

Christopher M. Spencer was born in 1841 and started making weapons at South Manchester, Connecticut, until he moved to Boston in about 1862. His design was a superb rapid-firing breechloader, feeding metallic cartridges from a tubular magazine inside the butt. The Spencer fired a .52 caliber rimfire straight copper cartridge, although as the case actually measured .56 inches in diameter, the cartridge is often referred to as the No. 56 or the .56-56. Cartridges are fed into the breech by cranking down the trigger guard lever.

While the Spencer carbines are better-known weapons, he used the same design principles to create full-length rifles. Similar to the carbine, the rifle has a longer, 30-inch, barrel and a full-length stock extending almost to the muzzle, with an iron tip and secured by three barrel bands. There were two almost identical variants, one for the navy (1,000 produced in 1862–4) the other for the army (11,450 produced in 1863–4). We show here two army rifles.

The basic Model 1816, in this case manufactured in 1826.

Springfield Models 1816/1840/1842

The Springfield Armory was one of two federal armories set up by George Washington's government, and first began the manufacture of flintlock smoothbore muskets in 1795. The later Models 1816, 1840 and 1842 were all based on this first musket, with only minor improvements between each model. They are all .69 caliber flintlock muskets, with 42-inch barrels; all are fitted for a bayonet and have three barrel bands.

Thousands of these weapons were later converted to the percussion mechanism and some had their smoothbore barrels rifled. Obsolete by the time of the Civil War, many still ended up as the used by soldiers of both sides who weren't fortunate enough to be issued with a more up-to-date piece.

SPECIFICATIONS	
Type: muzzleloading, flintlock musket	
Origin: National Armory, Springfield, Illinois	
Caliber: .69	
Barrel Length: 42 in	

Colonel Rush Hawkins and men from his "Hawkins Zouaves" regiment pose with their .69 caliber smoothbore Model 1842 muskets.

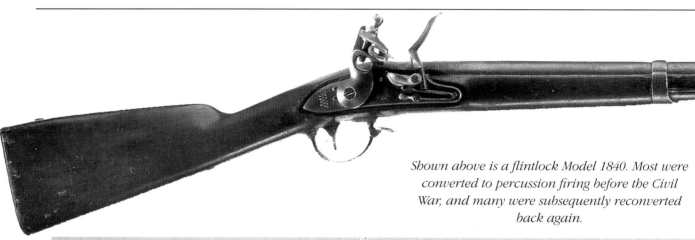

Shown above is a flintlock Model 1840. Most were converted to percussion firing before the Civil War, and many were subsequently reconverted back again.

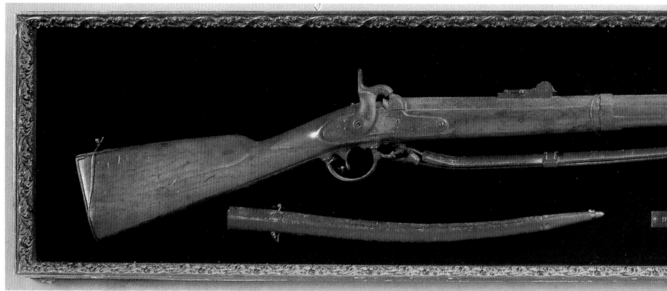

Probably one of the finest examples of the gun in existence.

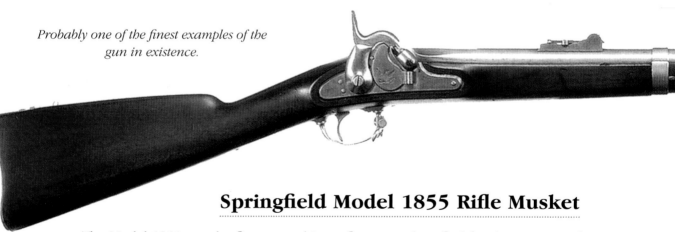

Springfield Model 1855 Rifle Musket

The Model 1855 was the first general issue firearm to be rifled for the .58 expanding Minie bullet. It was made at Springfield, Illinois and at the other federal armory at Harpers Ferry, Virginia (see entry above). Private contractors also manufactured the gun. The Model 1855 also used the Maynard Tape Priming system, and can be easily recognized by the high "hump" in the lockplate with its hinged door to give access to the tape compartment. Thousands of Model 1855s were used by both sides during the war, and we show two fine examples here.

*We have a very fine display comprising a Springfield Model 1842 musket, complete
with sling, bayonet and powder horn, and, for a reason not clear, a British
bayonet scabbard.*

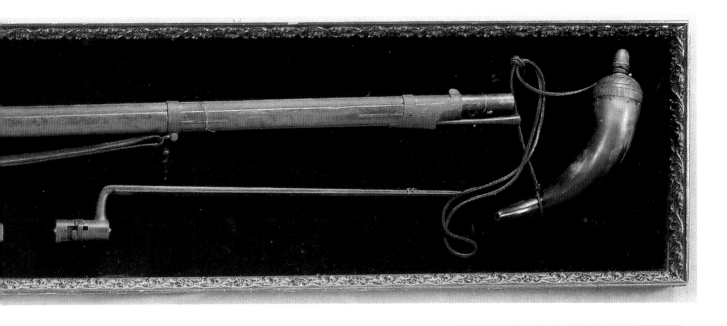

This Springfield lock is a work of art.

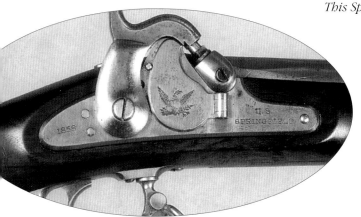

SPECIFICATIONS
Type: percussion rifle musket
Origin: National Armory, Springfield, Illinois
Caliber: .58
Barrel Length: 40 in

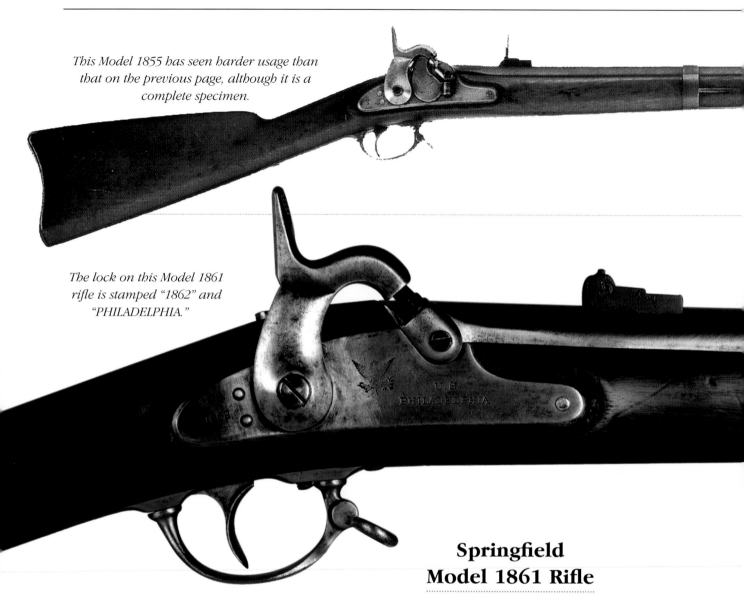

This Model 1855 has seen harder usage than that on the previous page, although it is a complete specimen.

The lock on this Model 1861 rifle is stamped "1862" and "PHILADELPHIA."

Springfield Model 1861 Rifle

Every so often, designers produce a weapon that gets everything "just right" for the times in which it operates and the wars it has to fight. Regarded by many as the most effective percussion muzzle-loading rifle ever produced, the Model 1861 Springfield Rifle was reliable, hard-hitting, well-balanced, reasonably light, and deadly effective in the right hands. Firing an expandable Minie bullet it was significantly more accurate and destructive at longer ranges than its predecessors. Over one million of this percussion rifle were produced during the Civil War years and it was the single type that saw the widest use in the conflict. Only the British Enfield series came close in the numbers of rifles in service.

Unlike the earlier Model 1855, the Model 1861 reverted to a copper percussion cap and nipple for priming and ignition of the main charge. The Maynard Tape system had turned out to be not as reliable as it needed to be in combat, being vulnerable to rain and damp conditions. Thousands of Model 1861s were also made by private contractors, and a selection are of shown here.

SPECIFICATIONS

Type: percussion rifle musket

Origin: National Armory, Springfield, Illinois

Caliber: .58

Barrel Length: 40 in

This sergeant from the 7th New York State Militia stands fully-equipped, and armed with a Model 1861 rifle-musket. His Springfield Rifle was a well balanced, light and effective weapon that proved popular with its users.

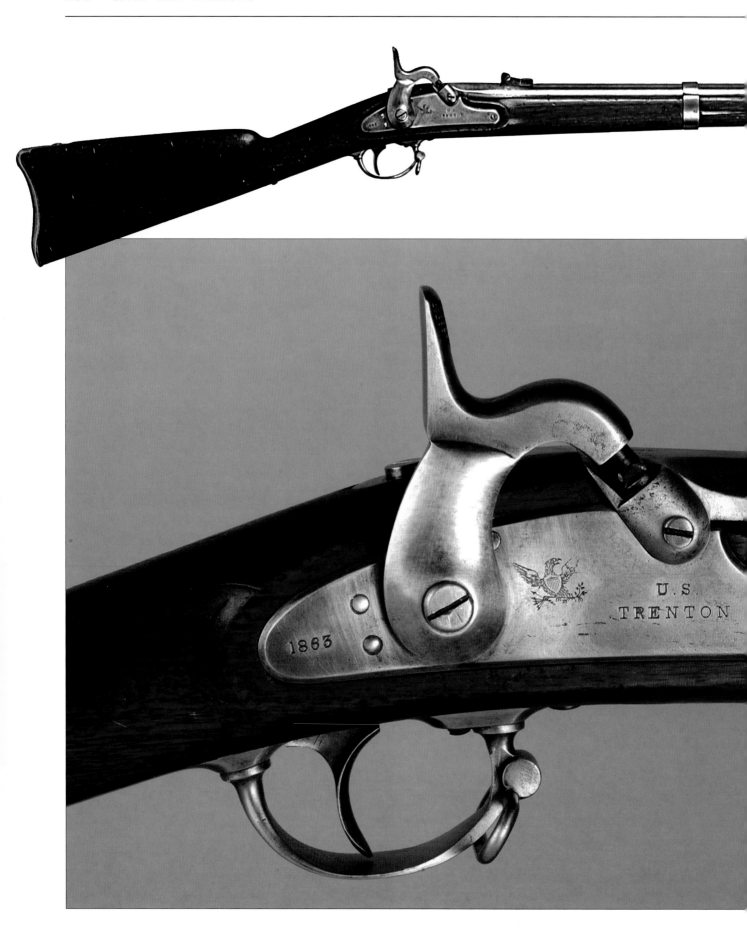

A fine Model 1861. The horizontal spring clips in front of the three barrel retaining bands were to prevent them working loose under the typical rough handling of life in the field.

Springfield Model 1861s were manufactured by numerous suppliers. The lockplate on the one on the left shows it was made by Trenton.

This Model 1861 was another contract one made at the Bridesburg Machine Works, Pennsylvania.

Springfield Model 1863

By 1863, Springfield was the only government arsenal under Union control (Harper's Ferry had been destroyed during a Confederate raid in 1961). The Model 1861 was a success, and both Springfield and various private contractors were producing rifles as fast as they could. The Union couldn't afford to interrupt production for a new design, but they did introduce a slight modification to the earlier rifle. Known as the Model 1863, the new rifle was effectively a Model 1861 with some minor improvements to the hammer and muzzle retaining bands. We show here a Model 1863 Type I.

SPECIFICATIONS

Type: percussion rifle musket

Origin: National Armory, Springfield, Illinois

Caliber: .58

Barrel Length: 40 in

The Provost Guard of the 107th Colored Infantry at Fort Corcoran, Washington D.C. with their Springfield Model 1863 rifle muskets.

The Model 1863 Type II had further modifications to the rearsight and spring retainers for the barrel bands.

"Piling" rifles into pyramid-style stacks was a common method of temporary storage in the field. The soldiers should be able to quickly grab their weapons if called for, although these men seem relaxed and don't appear to be worried by the likelihood of any nearby enemy.

Springfield Shotgun Conversion

When the Civil War ended, and men returned to their homesteads, the need was for shotguns for hunting and defense rather than military rifles.

Springfield Joslyn Rifle

Benjamin F. Joslyn was one of the seemingly inexhaustible supply of inventors with which America was blessed in the 19th century. He had many firearms patents to his credit, one of which led to this rifle, the first true breechloading weapon to be manufactured at the Springfield Armory and issued to the army. The device consisted of a cylindrical section, about two inches long, which fitted on to the end of the barrel. It was hinged on the left and was lifted by a knob to enable a cartridge to be inserted into the chamber, and then closed again. It was a simple and reliable system and 30,007 actions were bought in late 1864 and used in these rifles, which in other respects resembled the Springfield Model 1863 muzzle-loading rifle. Because the barrel was some 3 inches shorter than that for the Model 1863, the Joslyn rifle had a new bayonet, 2 inches longer, to maintain the infantryman's "reach." Approximately 50 percent of these rifles were converted to .50-70 centerfire and sold to the French army in 1870.

Many war surplus rifles were converted to such civilian use by retaining the percussion lock and trigger, replacing the barrel with a smoothbore one and cutting down the stock to suit. The one shown here is typical of the type, being based on Model 1842 Rifle Musket. In this way a trusted firearm could have a second career.

SPECIFICATIONS

Type: single-shot shotgun

Origin: National Armory, Springfield, Illinois

Caliber: .69

Barrel Length: 35.25 in

Virginia Manufactory First Model Rifle

The Virginia Manufactory (sometimes also known both as the Richmond Armory and the Virginia State Armory) was established in 1797 to produce weapons for the Virginia State Militia. Production took place between 1802 and 1820, when the building was turned over to be used as a school. The weapon seen here was the first design to be manufactured there and some 14,000 were completed between 1802 and 1809, and is typical of designs of the time. Many of these were still around at the time of the Civil War and were pressed into service by the Confederacy, usually with troops on secondary duties. The former Virginia Manufactory was also returned to its arms-making business in 1860 using machinery assembled from various sources. See also the earlier "Richmond Rifles" entry.

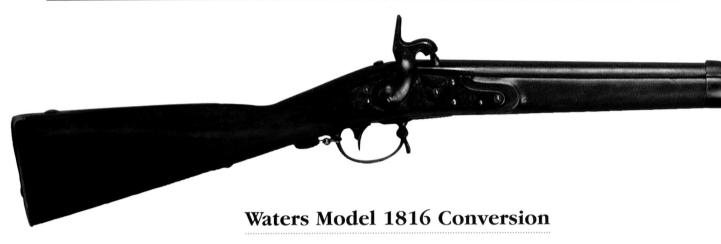

Waters Model 1816 Conversion

The Waters company made some 36,000 Model 1816 muskets under contract from 1817–36. As with most Model 1816s, many were later converted to percussion and were used during the Civil War. This one has "1830" on the lockplate and has been so converted. The detail shows the lockplate, which has been modified using the "Belgian" method. The frizzen and pan have been removed and a lump of brass inserted into the ensuing gap. Various fixing screws for the flintlock mechanism have also been ground down.

SPECIFICATIONS

Type: percussion musket

Origin: A. Waters Jr., Millbury, Massachusetts

Caliber: .69

Barrel Length: 42 in

Whitney Model 1822 Percussion Conversion

The Whitney company produced some 39,000 of these flintlock muskets from 1822 to 1841, based on the Model 1816 with minor modifications. Eli Whitney Sr.

Flintlock muskets had been around for some 200 years without significant developments until the percussion system proved its worth in terms of reliability and effectiveness.

The close-up shows how the Belgian conversion from flintlock worked. It was a crude but effective solution where the pan was ground off and a brass plug hammered into the resulting hole. The top of the barrel was drilled and tapped to accept the nipple.

died in 1824, before the first muskets were delivered, and the company was run for most of this time by Philos and Eli Whitney Blake, his nephews. The musket shown here is a Civil War one which has been converted to percussion firing using the "Belgian" method.

SPECIFICATIONS

Type: single-shot percussion musket

Origin: Whitneyville Armory, New Haven, Connecticut

Caliber: .69

Barrel Length: 42 in

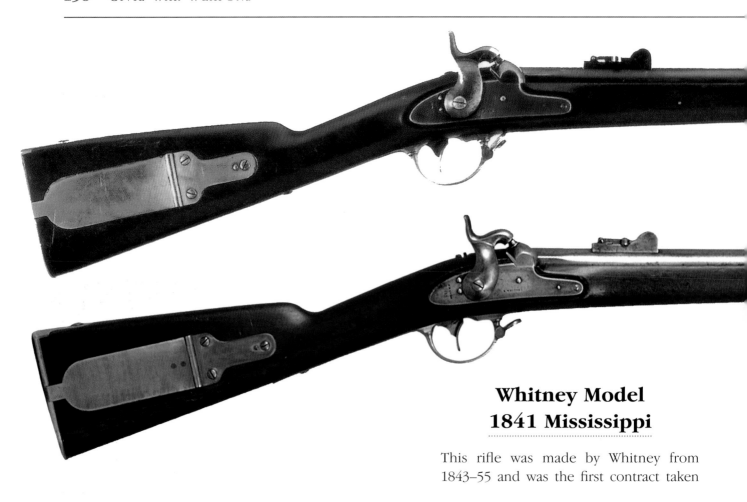

Whitney Model 1841 Mississippi

This rifle was made by Whitney from 1843–55 and was the first contract taken

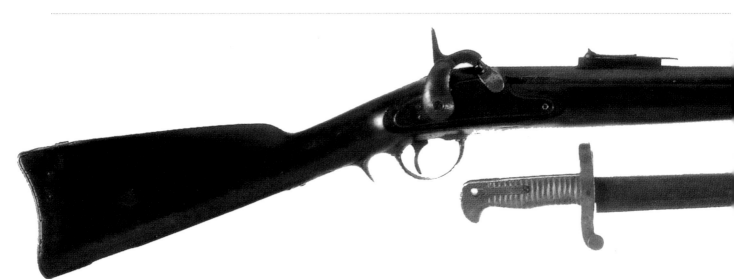

Whitney 1861 Navy Percussion (Plymouth Rifle)

This rifle was developed at the instigation of Captain John Dahlgren, an Ordnance officer for the U.S. Navy. Much of the development was undertaken on board the ordnance trials ship *USS Plymouth*, hence the name given to the rifle. Whitney delivered 10,000 of these rifles from 1861–64 and they proved to be accurate and effective. Note the large folding rearsight on this example.

A neat rifle, the Whitney Mississippi had a folding rearsight for long range fire.

up by Eli Whitney Jr. after he took over the company from the Blakes. It may have only had a 33-inch barrel, but as it was developed to fire the Minie expanding bullet it was effective and accurate at long ranges. Over 26,500 were delivered.

SPECIFICATIONS

Type: single-shot percussion rifle

Origin: Whitneyville Armory, New Haven, Connecticut

Caliber: .54

Barrel Length: 33 in

SPECIFICATIONS

Type: single-shot percussion musket

Origin: Whitneyville Armory, New Haven, Connecticut

Caliber: .69

Barrel Length: 34 in

This rifle comes complete with its original sword bayonet.

SPECIAL FEATURE

Hiram Berdan and his Distinguished Sharpshooters

At the outbreak of the Civil War, Hiram Berdan (September 6, 1824 – March 31, 1893) was a mechanical engineer living in New York City. He had a special interest in weapons, and is reputed to have invented a repeating rifle and a patented musket ball. His inventions included the specially adapted 1859 Berdan Sharps bolt-action rifle, which was to be so valuable in Union service during the war. Berdan was also a crack rifleman and had been the top amateur marksman in the United States since 1846. Always a great self-promoter, Berdan wrote to Secretary of War Edwin M. Stanton, suggesting the establishment of a corps of specially picked marksman to fight on the side of the Union. They were to be equipped with the best possible rifles, making them invaluable as sharpshooters and skirmishers. Stanton agreed the proposal and commissioned Berdan Colonel of the 1st Regiment on November 30, 1861. The marksmen were to be known as Berdan's Sharpshooters. Volunteers were advertised for, for this "distinguished branch of the service too well known for any comments" they were also invited to examine the "Improved

Hiram Berdan in military uniform. Although he received several brevets – finally attaining the honorary rank of Major General, his practical level of command remained as Colonel.

Sharp's hair trigger breech-loading rifle" with which they were to be equipped. Each applicant had to pass a shooting test, and had to put ten bullets in succession within a ten-inch circle at 200 yards at rest and 100 yards off hand, without the benefit of a telescopic sight. During the summer and fall of 1861, eighteen companies of United States Sharp-shooters were recruited from eight states and were formed into two regiments. Bounties were paid to enlisting men, $402 to Veteran Volunteers, and $302 to "all others."

The original recruits were also encouraged to bring their own target rifles, and were promised that the government would pay $60 for every suitable rifle, but this promise was never kept. Despite the reservations of the Ordnance Department, and Lincoln's cost concerns, the regiments were ultimately armed with Sharps breech-loading rifles. Although General Scott felt that the weapons would "spoil Berdan's command," and Lincoln was worried by the gun's price tag ($35 as opposed to $12 for a Springfield), their issue was finally approved when the Colt revolving rifle proved inadequate.

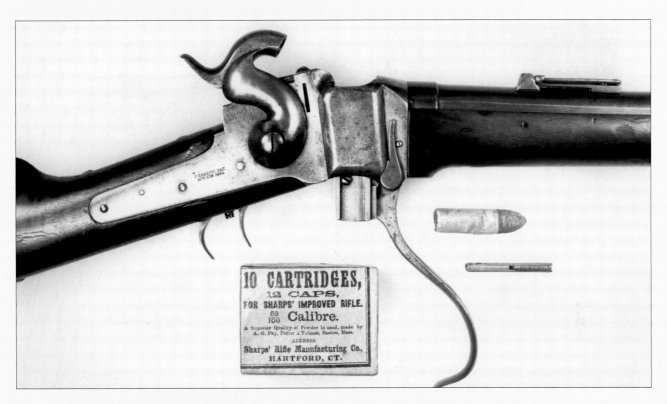

A closeup of the famous Sharps action and an original pack of ammunition.

An 1861 poster from Windham County, Vermont, challenging recruits to test their skills as Sharpshooters.

The 1st Regiment was formed from ten companies, A–K: four from New York, three from Michigan, one from New Hampshire, one from Vermont, and one from Wisconsin. Each company had a commanding captain. The 2nd Regiment had only eight companies, A---H: two from New Hampshire, two from Vermont, one from Minnesota, one from Michigan, one from Pennsylvania, and one from Maine. From September 1891 to March 1862, the chosen recruits were billeted at the U.S.S.S. (United States Sharp Shooters) "Camp of Instruction," which was situated north of Washington. Their tough training revolved around learning how to shoot effectively and economically, and to use cover as effectively as possible. All orders were given by bugle call.

The Sharpshooters' uniforms were highly distinctive. Their coats were made from a fine, dark

TO THE
SHARP SHOOTERS
OF WINDHAM COUNTY!

Your Country Calls!! Will you Respond?

CAPT. WESTON has been authorized to raise a Company of Green Mountain Boys for Col. Berdan's Regiment of Sharp Shooters which has been accepted by the War Department to serve for three years, or during the war. Capt. Weston desires to have Windham County represented in his Company.

The Sharp Shooters of Windham County and vicinity who are willing to serve their country in this time of need and peril, are requested to meet at the ISLAND HOUSE in Bellows Falls, on TUESDAY, the 27th inst., at 1 o'clock, P. M., for the purpose of testing their skill in TARGET SHOOTING. There are great inducements to join this celebrated Regiment, destined to be the most important and popular in the Service.

No person will be enlisted who cannot when firing at the distance of 200 yards, at a rest, put ten consecutive shots in a target, the average distance not to exceed five inches from the centre of the bull's eye to the centre of the ball.

GREEN MOUNTAIN BOYS!
"Rally for the support of the Stars and Stripes!"
YOU ARE INVITED TO BRING YOUR RIFLES.
F. F. STREETER, Supt. of Trial.
BELLOWS FALLS, VT., August 19, 1861.

Phenix Job Office, Bellows Falls.

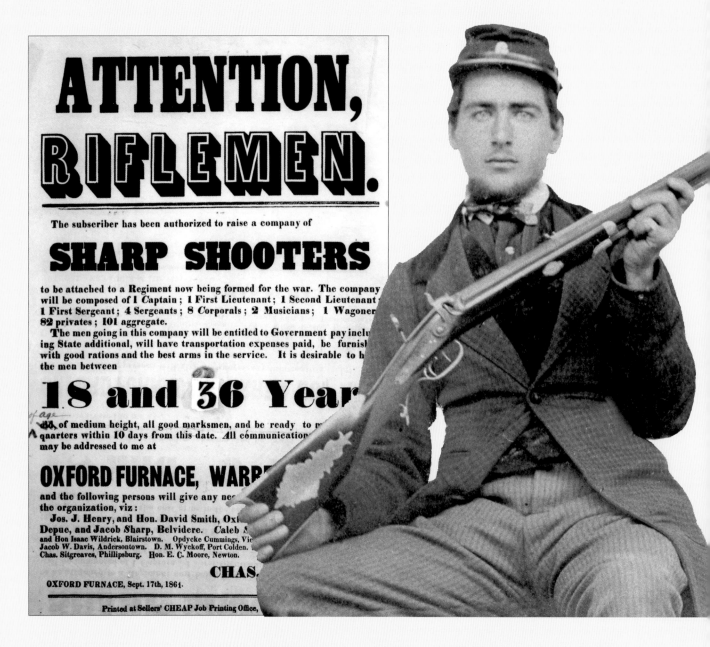

green cloth, as were their black-plumed caps. Originally, their trousers were light blue, but were later exchanged for green ones. They also had leather leggings, and hair-covered calfskin knapsacks that had a cooking kit attached to each one. Unsurprisingly, the Sharpshooters became known as the "Green Coats," and were considered to make a "handsome appearance." A New York Post correspondent said that the regiments reminded him of Robin Hood's outlaws.

As well as the distinctive uniform, each Sharpshooter was also issued with the following equipment: rifle, bayonet and scabbard, screwdriver,

Above left: A recruitment poster for Sharpshooter regiments promising "the best arms in the service."
Above right: In the early days of the regiment many recruits brought their own guns as shown here.
Right: Poster from Utica, New York, extolling the virtues of Berdan's improved Sharps rifle, and the green Sharpshooters' uniform.

cleaning thong and brush, leather sling, leather cartridge carrier, and leather cap pouch.

The U.S.S.S.'s first skirmish took place against enemy foragers at Lewinsville, Virginia in September 1861, and they ultimately took part in

COL. BERDAN'S REGIMENT OF
SHARP-SHOOTERS!

20 MORE RESPECTABLE MEN WANTED TO COMPLETE
CAPTAIN G. S. TUCKERMAN'S COMPANY!

Now stationed at NORTHERN HOTEL, Utica, N. Y.

"Many are called but few chosen."

This Company consists of gentlemanly men--none other need apply-- as it is the "Crack Regiment" in the Service.

OUR WAGES ARE HIGHER THAN ANY OTHER COMPANY'S!

As many furnish their own Rifles, but the Government supplies each man with one of Berdan's Improved Sharp's Rifle, which will fire 1 1-4 mile, at the rate of 18 times per minute. We have no drill but Skirmish Drill, no Picket duty; our manner of warfare is like the "Guerillas" or Indian. Our uniform is "Green" for summer, color of the grass and foliage, and "Miller's Grey" for fall and winter. You are privileged to lay upon the ground while shooting, picking your position; no commanders while fighting. I will pay board and traveling expenses as soon as enlisted.

H. L. HURLBUT!

Is the regular United States authorized recruiting officer for this Company, and will remain here for enlistments, at the

HOTEL,

GENTLEMEN--This is a beautiful chance for those wishing to see something of this life away from home. The $100 BOUNTY, LAND WARRANT, &c., same as in all other Regiments.

APPLY IN UTICA TO CAPT. TUCKERMAN, BAGG'S HOTEL.
Here to

Nov. 30, 1861.   H. L. HURLBUT.

Tough training encouraged the Sharpshooters to seek inventive positions to fire on the enemy. Even so, their aggressive stance often exposed them to heavy losses.

The Colt Revolving Rifle Model 1855 with advanced telescopic sight.

over sixty-five famous battles and actions. These included the advance on Yorktown, Virginia, the Battle of Williamsburg, the Battle of Antietam, the pursuit of Lee to Manassas Gap, Virginia, the Siege of Petersburg, Virginia, the Battle of Fredericksburg, and the "Mud March." The fact that Sharpshooters were normally deployed close to enemy positions meant that they suffered heavy losses during the war (a total of 532 to wounding and disease), and very few Sharpshooters became prisoners of war. Despite this, their morale was generally very high. Their dangerous and heroic work generated many legends and heroes, including dead shot "California Joe," and Lorenzo Barber, "The Fighting Parson." The 1st and 2nd Regiments of Sharpshooters claimed to have killed more Confederates than any other two regiments on the Union side.

Shortly after the outbreak of war, Berdan was breveted Brigadier General, United States Volunteers at Chancellorsville and was further promoted to Major General, United States Volunteers, for services rendered at the Battle of Gettysburg. This included a scout that he commanded personally on the second day of the battle. But in reality, these brevets were honorary and did not entitle him to command above the level of Colonel.

As time went by, Berdan became an increasingly controversial figure, too involved in the relative superiorities of various rifles, and in pursuing government contracts for his inventions. Indeed, it

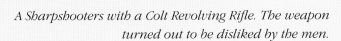

A Sharpshooters with a Colt Revolving Rifle. The weapon turned out to be disliked by the men.

In one of the most famous images of the Sharpshooters, Private Truman Head, nicknamed "California Joe," takes cover behind a convenient rock, Sharps at the ready.

was said of him that he was more often seen in a parlor than a rifle pit. Both military and civilian contemporaries became antagonistic towards him, believing him to be self-interested, unscrupulous, and unfit for command. His own men became highly critical of his personal ambition and unseemly avoidance of the enemy at all costs –

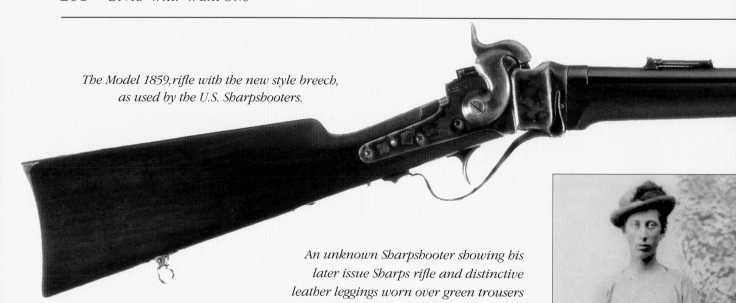

The Model 1859, rifle with the new style breech, as used by the U.S. Sharpshooters.

An unknown Sharpshooter showing his later issue Sharps rifle and distinctive leather leggings worn over green trousers

allegations of cowardice, in fact. Day-to-day command of the Sharpshooters was substantially devolved onto the shoulders of Lt. Col. Frederick Mears. Berdan ultimately resigned his commission on January 2, 1864 to pursue his other interests. He went on to develop a twin-screw submarine gunboat, a torpedo boat for evading torpedo nets, a long-distance range finder, and a distance fuze for shrapnel.

Berdan died in 1893, and was buried in Section 2 of Arlington National Cemetery.

The Colt 5-shot revolving rifle

Berdan's Sharpshooters were undoubtedly the most famous Civil War unit to be equipped with the Colt revolving rifle, as Berdan was always at the forefront of equipping his men with more advanced armaments than the standard army issue. Supported by President Lincoln, he received 1,000 Colts from the Ordnance Department. However, the weapons were not as successful as had been anticipated, and were soon replaced with the Sharps. In fact, although Colt had been one of the first arms manufacturers to anticipate that the market for revolving rifles would ultimately be more important than that for pistols, his Model 1855 Military Rifle (in .44 and .56 caliber), and his Model 1855 Revolving Carbine were jointly responsible for only 13,700 units manufactured during the Civil War. This was just a tiny fraction of the weapons required by the Northern forces.

The short sighted Ordnance Department was somewhat to blame for this limited introduction of the Colt, as they were less than enthusiastic about repeating rifles. But the real problem for the gun was that the Spencer and Henry equivalents were actually better and more reliable systems.

Colt's Civil War rifle production was therefore concentrated on single-shot .58 caliber rifle muskets (of the type adopted by the Springfield Armory). Springfield contracted out and produced over 500,000 examples of this weapon, while Colt delivered 75,000 units.

Berdan's regiments of Sharpshooters reluctantly accepted the Colts on the basis that these would be replaced by Sharps as soon as these became available. The Colt had a distressing tendency to discharge all of its cylinders at once, which led to some horrific injuries to their users, and they were gladly handed in when the Sharps were introduced in 1862.

Private John Page of Company F, 1st U.S. Sharpshooters with his Sharps at the ready.

The Sharps Model 1859 Rifle for Berdan's Sharpshooters

Berdan had always intended that his men should be equipped with Sharps rifles (named after their creator, Christian Sharps), and he cooperated with the company to make several valuable modifications to the gun (without permission from the Ordnance Department). These included the introduction of the angular bayonet (which made a bayonet lug redundant), the modification of the rear sight to improve long-distance accuracy (at up to 1,000 yards), and the replacement of the single trigger with the double-set trigger (which was borrowed from the Sharps sporting rifles).

The initial order for 2,000 guns (supplied at $42.50 each, including bayonets) was delivered to the grateful Sharpshooters in 1862. The Sharps were delivered to the 1st Regiment in May, and to the 2nd in June. The guns carried the serial numbers 54374 to 57567, but this range also includes around 1,300 Sharps M1859 carbines and a number of single trigger non-Berdan M1859 rifles. The guns were light (at 8 pounds, 12 ounces), compact (47 inches long overall), accurate, and rapid (capable of up to nine rounds per minute). They gave their users immediate satisfaction and were highly valued by the Sharpshooters, becoming known as their "truthful Sharps." The weapon used a .52 caliber conical lead ball, with skin or linen cartridges (containing 64 grains of black powder), and was equipped to use Lawrence Pellet primers. The men themselves often preferred the original "hat" percussion caps. As a breechloader, the firearm was capable of being loaded in the prone position, which was ideal for the Sharpshooters. Each man carried 40 rounds in his ammunition box, and 20 more in his knapsack. 100 rounds were issued when action was imminent.

Although Berdan came under a hail of criticism from his own men, for military incompetence and alleged cowardice, it was his business and political connections that made the issue of Sharps guns to the Sharpshooters possible. Weapons that they made the most of and came to value so highly.

CHAPTER FOUR

Artillery

As with other weaponry, the Civil War gave a huge impetus to the development of artillery technology and tactics. Before the war, however, the artillery branch was by far the smallest in the army; an underfunded "Cinderella" unpopular with most West Point graduates. Service with the guns was

As the war progressed, Confederate artillerymen had to deal with shortages off all kinds. Ingenuity and improvisation helped overcome this, such as with these dummy guns made from logs at Centreville, Virginia. From a distance these looked real enough, and could intimidate an attacking force into staying in their own trenches. For a while.

seen as lacking the excitement, glamor and opportunities for promotion of the infantry and cavalry. Cannon were also expensive to make and required high-quality industrial facilities, such that when the regular army split apart in April 1861, the artillery branch of the United States comprised only 48 batteries of four or six guns, while only a

few states had artillery militia units of their own

Although production on both sides was quickly stepped up as war began, recruitment continued to be difficult. As with their peacetime predecessors, most of the men who rallied to the colors again preferred the excitement and glamor of the infantry and cavalry. Artillery units needed a special type of man, one with technical aptitude as well as some mathematical education and ability. These qualities had to be combined with the cold courage necessary to work methodically on the complex interconnected tasks of the gun crew while shot and shell landed about them. But the importance of the big guns was unanswerable, and the size of the artillery arm on both sides quickly grew, as did its reputation and professionalism.

Civil War Artillery was divided into two main groupings, namely field and heavy artillery. Field artillery batteries, as the name suggests, were mobile units that accompanied the armies into battle, able to move with the infantry or cavalry they supported, and to set up and be ready to fire within minutes. Within the field artillery, descriptions such as light artillery, mounted artillery, horse artillery or even flying artillery were used.

Heavy artillery was the name given to larger pieces, normally emplaced in static positions to defend key points such as fortresses, harbours, major towns and other valuable locations. Some heavy artillery was movable and could be deployed as a "siege train" to provide a powerful bombardment force for a besieging army.

All the guns in use at the start of the war were smoothbore muzzleloaders, firing a range of projectiles including solid shot, explosive shell and

A neat battery of guns at Fort Marshall, Sullivan's Island, South Carolina. The nearest one, on the wheeled carriage, is lighter than most static defensive weapons, but can still cause a fearsome amount of damage.

multi-projectile rounds such as grapeshot and canister. As the war progressed, rifled pieces became more common, as did a host of different designs of shell intended to be used in such pieces. But loading by the muzzle remained the method of choice for almost all the guns that fought, and unlike small arms such as the cavalry carbine, the widespread use of breechloading cannon didn't occur until after the war.

Artillery in the field

The standard field artillery unit was the company or battery, commanded by a captain. Batteries were nominally grouped in regiments, but for all practical purposes this was ignored, and the battery on campaign was treated as in independent command. Union field batteries normally had six guns, and Confederate batteries four, but in both armies the numbers varied considerably from unit

Overleaf: Gunners had to be a special breed indeed. To carry out complex gun drills quickly and smoothly while shot and shell rained down about you took a particularly cold form of courage.

to unit, partly owing to the vagaries of combat, and partly to the difficulties of supply and manufacture. The Union tended to form a battery up to full strength then send it into combat, while the Confederacy often formed their batteries with one or two guns, then built up the strength with further deliveries over time.

In the early years of the war, batteries would have a mixture of guns and howitzers, perhaps four of the former (normally 6-pounders) and two of the latter (often 12-pounders). The guns were used for low-angle direct fire while the howitzers were lighter, and allowed for high-angled fire over the top of obstacles and fortifications. As the war progressed, it was found that the popular 12-pounder "Napoleon" gun-howitzers could fulfil both roles, and many batteries became equipped with this as a single type.

Field guns and howitzers were mounted on wooden wheeled carriages, and their ready-use ammunition was kept in wooden chests mounted on light carriages known as limbers. The gun would be hooked up to the limber and the whole assembly pulled by a six- or four-horse team. Batteries normally had another type of two-wheeled ammunition cart, or caisson, which was attached by a pole to the limber to form a four-wheeled combination. The amount of available ammunition varied depended on the size of the gun, but a 12-pounder gun may have had up to 96 rounds in its ammunition chests.

A single gun crew at full strength was either seven or eight men, and a six-gun battery may have up to 150–160 men, nearly a third of the whom were responsible for driving the horses who pulled the guns and the ammunition, supply and maintenance carts. Usually only the drivers and officers traveled on horseback, although the gun crews could sit on the limbers for short periods. Specialized fast-moving horse artillery batteries that supported cavalry units were usually all mounted, and the men in these units also carried sidearms such as revolvers, carbines or musketoons.

This neatly arrayed 6-pounder Wiard was one of those defending Washington from the attack that never came. The photograph shows the ram and sponge attached to the gun carriage and the limber and ammunition chest to the rear.

*Supplies of union artillery and ammunition pile up in harbor at City Point, Virginia.
Note the mortars in the foreground and stacks of spherical projectiles stacked up in a
neat pile. An array of Parrot rifles and their limbers is lined up behind the fence.*

This photograph is claimed to show an artillery unit on the battlefield, just about to go into action. The 12-pounder Napoleon cannon are arrayed in a neat row in the open, with their crews bustling around getting them ready to fire. The horses, carts and drivers can be seen to the rear.

The battery normally fought as a unit, although guns could be detached as independent pairs or sections in smaller actions. As the war progressed, both sides tended to concentrate their artillery into larger groupings, where several batteries might be attached to a division under a senior artillery commander. In some cases artillery reserves were created at corps or even army level.

The guns themselves would be deployed on the battlefield in a closely packed row, wheelhubs spaced a few yards apart. Sometimes multiple batteries were combined into a larger concentrated force. In a mobile battle this deployment would be quick, with the horse teams galloping forward into position and the men running alongside to get the

guns into action as quickly as possible. Once the guns were in place, the limber would be set up a few yards to the rear, with the ready-use ammunition to hand. The other carts and the horses would be sent further to the rear, hopefully out of enemy fire. A well-trained unit could have the guns ready to fire within a minute or two of the lead horses galloping onto the chosen firing position.

Heavy artillery

The term heavy artillery was given to the larger guns, and the units who manned them in the static fortresses and redoubts which sprang up around major cities, ports and other key positions. Batteries of heavy guns varied enormously in organisation, some even only having the one piece. With sizes ranging from 18- to 42-pounders, some of these monsters weighed well over 50 tons, and were often mounted on fixed metal or wooden carriages, occasionally fitted into curved rails at the

Heavy artillery could be put on to wheeled carriages and moved laboriously to take part in static siege operations. Their heavy projectiles were essential to batter down earthworks and fortifications.

rear of the mount to allow the guns to be traversed in place. Slow to reload (perhaps only capable of 12–20 shots per hour) they were nevertheless formidable threats to warships and attacking forces, especially as the guns themselves were protected by extensive earthworks or brick and stone casemates.

Some heavy weapons were also moved (with great difficulty) by rail or sea to take part in static siege operations, where an attacking army had the time to build protective emplacements for them and the transport to shift the guns and their large stocks of their ammunition. Heavy mortars were also extensively used in static battles, again being moved by rail or sea.

Union heavy artillery spent much of the war away from the action, and some gunner units even found themselves re-roled as infantry. However, fear of a Confederate attack on the capital tied down hundreds of guns, large stocks of ammunition and thousands of men in the forts and defenses around Washington.

A battery of heavy 13-inch mortars at Yorktown, VA. Note how they are placed out of the line of fire, ready to hurl their 200-pound projectiles over the log and earth wall in front of them. Some of these shells can be seen behind the nearest mortar.

Confederate heavy artillerymen had a much livelier time of it, finding themselves in some of the most important siege operations of the war, such as at Vicksburg, or the Federal siege of Fort Sumter and others, while also defending against naval attacks like that in Mobile Bay.

Naval guns

While there were no large ship-to-ship naval battles during the war, there were actions such as that between the armored monitors *Monitor* and *Merrimac*, the hunting of the Confederate commerce raider *Alabama*, and union attacks on coastal towns and fortresses. Both sides also made use of smaller ships and boats for river transport, and to provide firebases for bombardment. As naval guns didn't need to be moved by road, they tended to be larger than many land-based guns, and fired heavy shot, explosive shell, and grapeshot.

How the guns were made

As the war began, almost all the guns in use were smoothbore muzzleloading pieces, similar to those that had been in service around the world for many years. Most were cast from bronze, a heavy material, but tough enough to absorb the stresses of firing, and still light enough to allow mobile guns to mounted on wooden large-wheeled carriages.

As the war progressed, rifling became incorporated in the design of guns, increasing their range, accuracy and effectiveness, if at the cost of rate of fire. But bronze was too soft for rifling, the grooves being stripped out after a few shots. Cast iron appeared to be an obvious alternative, being lighter and harder, but unfortunately this very hardness made for a brittle weapon that over time became likely to burst in an explosion disastrous to those around it. Various methods were tried to

The green bloom on this line of memorial guns standing at Gettysburg is typical of bronze after exposure to the elements. This soft, yet tough, alloy was the most common material used to make guns in the early years of the war.

The remains of a shattered 300-pounder Parrot rifle at Morris Island, South Carolina, graphically shows the problems of cast iron construction. In this case the reinforcing band around the breech has held, but the gun has burst near the muzzle.

A 3-in Ordnance Rifle in front of a row of limbers and caissons, guarded by a sole infantryman. New methods of welding together iron rods made for a superbly strong, light and effective rifled artillery piece, probably the best of the war.

reinforce such guns, and that devised by Robert Parrott, where a wrought iron band was clamped around the breech, was the most widely used.

A later technique for producing a light, strong iron gun was developed, which incorporated layers of wrought iron welded together in strips and wrapped around a tubular shape to create a strong rifled piece. It was used to great effect in the 3in Ordnance Rifle, one of the best field guns of the war.

The use of steel was in its infancy, although the Wiard rifle made use of a form of wrought iron known as "semi-steel." The few true steel guns that fought in the war were the British Whitworth and Armstrong rifles imported by the Confederacy, and which provided spectacular accuracy and long range. Such advanced breechloading designs didn't stand up to the rigors of combat as well as their muzzle-loading brethren, and the concept didn't find widespread military acceptance until after the war.

Ammunition

Any survey of artillery ammunition of the war should begin with the solid metal sphere. Cast from iron, they had been the standard "cannonball" for hundreds of years, and were still the standard field projectile as the war broke out. Fired by such cannon as the 6-pounder and the "Napoleon" 12-pounders, their main attraction was that they were cheap, simple and easy to make. They were also easy to handle and load in the stresses of battle. Their effectiveness was limited against well-made fortifications or dispersed troops, although they could cut a swathe of destruction through tightly packed infantry and cavalry formations.

Elongated solid shot was also used by rifled weapons, although here the projectiles were referred to as bolts. They same considerations of cheapness and ease of manufacture apply here, while their greater penetrative power made them more effective against fortifications, earthworks and static defenses.

Explosive shells were also extensively fired by both smoothbore and rifled weapons. The simplest were a hollow casing packed with powder, ignited by a simple time fuze, although some had a shaped cavity with sharp edges which encouraged the projectile to burst into regularly sized fragments. Their time fuzes were a train of powder, sometimes wrapped in paper, and held in a metal or wooden

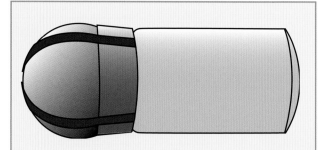

A smoothbore 12-pounder round. Metal straps hold the iron shot to the wooden base or "sabot," while a cloth bag tied to the back contains the powder. The sabot and shot separate as they leave the barrel, while the bag is burnt away.

This image of Charleston demonstrates the destructive power of heavy artillery. The city was heavily shelled by naval guns and by heavy Parrot rifles on Morris Island.

Some idea of the amount of ammunition a gun battery can consume can be gained from this array of neatly stacked cannonballs at the Washington Arsenal.

plug that was ignited by the firing of the gun. This powder burned at a controlled rate until the flame reached the main bursting charge, causing the projectile to explode.

Rifled projectiles impacted nose first, so percussion fuzing was also possible. In this case the

fuze had some form of striker which was pushed into a percussion cap by the impact on the target. This percussion cap exploded, sending a small flame through a tube which ignited the main charge, much in the same way as contemporary musket.

Case shot was a more elaborate design of explosive shell. Such projectiles had a thinner shell wall and were packed with small lead or iron balls, and with a smaller bursting charge in the centre. The bursting charge was normally detonated by a time fuze, and would send a deadly spray of balls and shell fragments around the impact area. The concept was invented by the British artillery officer, Henry Shrapnel, and such shells are often referred to as shrapnel shells. Fragmenting explosive shells were effective against all kinds of targets, while shrapnel was deadly against infantry, cavalry or gun batteries in the open.

The third main class of shell fired multiple projectiles. Canister, as its name suggests, was a thin-walled metal tin packed with iron or lead balls held in sawdust. When fired it sprayed these balls

Dead horses and wrecked carriages at Fredericksburg, Virginia, attest to the power of a 32-pounder shell.

The men may be infantrymen posing for the photographer, but the gun is a static fortress piece at Fort Corcoran. Note the pile of grapeshot projectiles in front of the soldiers.

out from the muzzle like a huge shotgun blast, and was deadly at close range against personnel. Grape shot had larger balls and no casing, the balls usually held together by fabric or metal rings. Grape shot was much more commonly used by naval guns or by coastal defence units, but was also sometimes seen on land.

Smoothbore ammunition normally came as a single "round", comprising three elements. At the front was the projectile, either spherical solid shot or explosive shell, or perhaps a cylindrical canister. Behind a spherical shell, and attached to it with metal straps, was normally a wooden base or "sabot." The sabot helped provide a gas seal when the gun was fired, then would fly off once the projectile had left the barrel, leaving the shot or shell to continue to the target. Behind the sabot and tied to it was a cylindrical cloth bag holding a couple of pounds of black powder propellant, and the bag would be consumed when charge ignited. Muzzle-loading rifled weapons normally had tighter-fitting projectiles, so the charge and shell were loaded and rammed separately, giving a slightly slower rate of fire.

Putting a spin on it

Making the projectile longer than a sphere and spinning it before it left the barrel were well-known methods of increasing the range, accuracy and effectiveness of a firearm, and during the war the same principles were applied to artillery. Some pre-war smoothbore cannon were converted by engraving grooves into the barrel in a spiral pattern, although those made from bronze soon wore out this rifling. Other rifled cannon were designed and made from new. Most of these were still muzzle-loaders, so a mechanism had to be devised which allowed the shell or bolt to be rammed down the barrel, but enabled it to engage tightly with the rifling grooves when fired.

Parrott shells (and their close relative, the Read-Parrott) were the most common rifled projectiles. These had a ring or cup of soft metal on the base of the shell made from brass, copper, lead or wrought

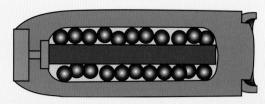

A cutaway of a Parrott shrapnel shell, showing the shell casing, the time fuze, a narrow bursting charge in the centre and the lead or iron balls. At the rear the lead or copper cup-shaped disc is pushed out to engage the rifling.

Whitworth projectiles had angled facets to engage with the hexagonal section barrel.

The Schenkl system used a wooden or paper mache sabot over the tapered "boat-tail."

iron. Gas pressure on firing caused this ring to expand, pressing it into the grooves to engage with them and form a gas seal at the same time.

Many other methods were used. For example, Hotchkiss shells were made in two parts, held together by soft lead sabot ring. The shock of firing drove the base part of the shell into the forward bursting part, forcing this sabot outwards into the rifling. Other projectiles had nib-like projections that engaged in the grooves, while the Schenkl designs had distinctive curved and tapered section behind the main part of the shell. Surrounding this was a sabot, usually made from paper mache or sometimes wood. On firing, the gas pressure forced this sabot up the tapered section causing it to expand and engage the rifling.

The 8-man crew gather around this superbly maintained 100-pounder Parrott rifle at Fort Corcoran while another group are encouraged to pose on top of the fortress walls.

Attempts were also made to impart spin to shells fired by smoothbore weapons but none were particularly effective. Some used a carefully shaped nose with angled raised and lowered elements, such that the air pressure as it flew caused the shell to rotate slightly. Other designs used spring-loaded fins or vanes for the same effect.

A pound of what?

The terminology used to describe the size of guns and the power of their shot was inconsistent and confusing, and remains so today. In the days of solid shot, the terminology used to name a cannon described the weight of a spherical iron ball that would fit that gun. For example, an iron sphere of about 3.67 in diameter would weigh close to 6

pounds, so guns of that caliber were known as 6-pounders. A 12-pounder gun had a bore of about 4.62 in. All fairly clear and understandable – until the advent of rifled cannon.

Rifled guns used many different designs of projectile, but the one thing they had in common was that they were longer than spherical, thus removing the relationship between barrel diameter and weight of projectile. For instance, during the war many 6-pounders were rifled, having their barrel diameter enlarged slightly from 3.67 to 3.8 in during the process. They now fired a longer shell significantly heavier than its spherical predecessor so the modified gun was now often referred to as a 12-pounder.

In theory rifled cannon were designated by their bore diameter, but in practice it was less consistent than that. The Parrott weapons, for instance, were made in a range of calibers, and were still usually referred to by the weight of shell. So the 8-inch Parrot rifle was known as the 200-pounder by the army. When the original projectile was redesigned to be shorter, it weighed in at only 150 pounds so the navy used designation 150-pounder, even though the army stayed with 200-pounder.

Even more confusing was the Parrott 10-pounder series, which were manufactured at different times with two different sizes of bore (2.9- or 3-in). And as with all rifled guns, they fired a variety of projectile types with widely varying weights. Even so, the guns themselves are usually referred to as 10- or sometimes 12-pounders.

Firing the gun

A full-strength gun crew was normally eight men, although some guns had only seven. Each man was referred to by a number, and each carried out a specific function. Described here is how a typical field gun crew would work, although the principles were the same for larger pieces.

Once the gun had been rolled into a firing position, the limber was placed just to the rear then the horses and drivers withdrew further back, ideally out of the line of fire. The man in charge of the piece, the gunner (usually a corporal), would stand behind the gun and aim it, calling out the range and giving the loading commands.

On his command, crewmen 6 and 7 at the limber prepared the shells, cutting the time fuze in the right place to give the correct delay for the range called by the gunner. The number 5 then took take a round (shell, sabot and charge) from them and ran forward with it to give to the number 2, who stood alongside the left side of the muzzle (looking forward). The number 2 then inserted the complete round, charge first, into the barrel. The number 1, on the other side of the muzzle, stepped forward and drove the round down the barrel with the long rammer pole.

During this loading process crew member 3 kept his thumb over the firing vent to prevent any accidental ignition. Now he aimed the gun under the gunner's instructions, using a handspike to adjust the direction. At the same time the gunner adjusted the elevating screw to the estimated range,

During the loading process, the number 3 crewman kept his thumb (often protected by a leather patch) over the firing vent to prevent accidental ignition. Once the round was loaded he would then stick a metal pin through this vent to release some powder from the charge bag before the number 4 inserted the primer into the vent.

Crewman number 1 had to use a rammer to push the round right down the tube until it was firmly in the firing chamber. After the gun had fired, he'd reverse the ram to the sponge end, soak it in water from a leather bucket then swab any remaining cloth or powder residue from inside the barrel.

The crew of this 12-pounder bronze Napoleon is momentarily static for the photo-grapher before launching into the carefully choreographed pattern of actions necessary to keep their gun in action. A good crew could fire two or three rounds a minute for short periods.

using both his skill and experience and printed range tables to judge the elevation necessary.

At the command "Ready," the number 3 stuck a long metal pin through the firing vent to prick the charge bag and release some powder. The number 4 then inserted a friction primer into the vent ready for the final command. The primer was a thin metal tube filled with priming compound and with a twisted, serrated wire piece protruding from the top. The tube was fitted into the vent, then the gunner's lanyard tied into the loop of twisted wire. When the gunner gave the command "Fire", number 4 tugged this lanyard to pull the wire from the primer tube. The friction from this caused sparks which ignited the primer in the tube, and the ensuing flame passed down the tube into the main charge to fire the gun.

Once the gun had fired, the number 1 switched is rammer around to the sponge end and quickly swabbed out the barrel to clear any burning powder or cloth residue from the barrel while the next round was coming up from the ammunition chest.

The drill had to be rapid and slick, and gun crews spent hours practising it over and over again. A good crew could get two or three rounds per minute from a field gun, and often the limiting factor was the time taken to get the gun back into position and on aim after the recoil had pushed it backwards on its wheeled carriage.

And the drill had be so ingrained that the crew would work just as smoothly in the noise and smoke of battle, when enemy riflemen and artillery were shooting at them. And every man had to be able to do the job of others in the crew, so that the gun would continue to fire even when men were being killed and wounded around them.

Spotting from the air

Another technological first in this war was the use of aerial balloons for reconnaissance and artillery spotting. The first attempt by the Union to make use of a balloon ended in failure though, as it broke free from its tethers and had to be shot down to prevent it drifting across the lines in Confederate hands.

Aeronaut Thaddeus Lowe was tasked with forming a balloon corps in August 1862 after a demonstration to President Lincoln. The first American purpose-built military balloon, *"Union,"* began operations in the Washington area at the end of August, where Lowe immediately provided intelligence on Confederate troops massing nearby.

Another aeronaut, John LaMountain had also carried out aerial reconnaissance missions independently of Lowe, and the two men became bitter rivals for government funding and support. Lowe had better access to influential backers, such that LaMountain was eventually dismissed from service.

The Union force grew to seven balloons, all eventually using hydrogen to give them their lift. At first Lowe used a mixture of hot air and coal gas, but as there were no facilities for producing this in the field, he was forced to operate near urban gas lines in the Washington area. But once a mobile hydrogen gas generator had been built, the balloons provided tactical reconnaissance in a number of key battles, including the siege of Yorktown, and at Fredericksburg in 1863.

Lowe's balloons were flown tethered and had a telegraph system that allowed the balloonist to immediately send reports down to the ground. On September 24, 1861, while Lowe was operating near Arlington, Virginia, he sent detailed and regular reports on Confederate troops amassing a few miles away at Falls Church, Virginia. Based on these reports, Union artillery fired a long-range bombardment at troops they

Above: Thaddeus Lowe's "Intrepid" being filled with hydrogen before taking off to observe the battle of Fair Oaks, Virginia. Using telegraph wire to send messages to the ground, Lowe was able to guide Union artillery fire onto targets out of sight of the guns

Above left: Mobile balloon operations only became possible with the manufacture of these carts containing apparatus able to produce hydrogen gas in the field.

couldn't see, and which was guided onto target from information from Lowe. This was the first instance of accurate indirect artillery fire directed by a remote spotter, and Lowe became the first Artillery Forward Observation Officer in the history of warfare.

Another landmark was when one of Lowe's balloons was operated from a converted river barge – the first ever aircraft carrier.

But many senior officers had doubts about the value of balloons, believing their reports could be misleading and that the money and resources spent on them was a waste. Ulysses S. Grant was one such, and when he took over the Army of the Potomac he disbanded the Balloon Corps in August 1863.

The Confederacy also attempted to make use of aerial reconnaissance, and in 1862 built a cotton balloon which used hot air for lift. Under the command of Captain John Ryan this balloon provided intelligence reports over Yorktown, although on its second flight the tether was cut and the balloon drifted free. Ryan was then shot at by his own side, and it seems that even then, poor aircraft recognition by ground troops was a problem for airmen!

Later Confederate balloons were gas-filled and made from silk, including the legendary "Silk Dress Balloon" flown at Richmond, Virginia.

Model 1841 6-Pounder Field Gun

This was one of the U.S. Army's standard field guns from the 1840s onwards, although by the time of the war it was about to be superseded as the weapon of choice by the more powerful Model 1857 12-pounder. However, hundreds of 6-pounders served with both armies, and it was the most common field gun in use in the first year of the war, especially with the Confederacy. The Model 1841 had a bronze smoothbore tube of about 60 inches long, with a diameter of 3.67 inches, and could fire a solid shot to about 1,500 yards. The small projectile was relatively ineffective against any kind of fortification, and lost much of its energy by about 1,000 yards. As they became replaced by more powerful weapons the Union's 6-pounders were relegated to reserves or in some cases put onboard small river boats as improvised naval guns. The Confederacy couldn't spare the metal so many of their obsolete guns were melted down to make more modern weapons.

Model 1841 12-Pounder Howitzer

Lighter and more mobile than the Model 1841 6-pounder gun, the howitzer was effective at close range, firing either slid shot or shell. One or two were normally present in a field battery at the beginning of the war, although they were also sometimes grouped together into all-howitzer batteries. Once the effectiveness of the Model 1857 "Napoleon" became apparent the howitzer was replaced in many batteries.

The pre-war Model 1841 light howitzer had a much shorter, lighter barrel than the 6-pounder gun, and most field batteries had one or two in their order of battle.

Model 1857 "Napoleon" 12-Pounder Gun-Howitzer

Eventually becoming the most common (and most famous) field gun of the conflict, only four Model 1857s were in service as war broke out. The new design incorporated the best aspects of European guns, especially those inspired by Emperor Louis Napoleon III of France, hence the nickname "Napoleon" guns.

As a 12-pounder, it was significantly more powerful than the earlier Model 1841 6-pounder gun, even though it managed to remain reasonably

A fine view of Napoleon 12-pounders in fixed positions. The distinctive muzzle swell is an identifying feature for these effective smoothbore muzzleloaders, the most widely used field gun of the war.

The patina of age shows off the outline of this bronze 12-pounder Napoleon, at Cemetery Ridge in the Gettysburg National Park, near to the statue of General Meade. The guns have long been silent, but the exploits and courage of their crews still echo through history.

light and mobile. It could fire almost all types of smoothbore ammunition, including shot, shell, shrapnel, canister and grapeshot, and the maximum effective range was around 2,000 yards.

The gun was so effective that it was meant to replace the Model 1841 guns and howitzers, although these older weapons actually remained in

This illustration shows the culmination of Pickett's charge at Gettysburg, with the Confederates getting to grips with the Union defenders. The reinforcing band around the breech of the gun identifies it as a 10-pounder Parrott rifle.

service for quite some time. Made from bronze, around 1,200 were produced for the Union in five different foundries. The Confederacy had them in large numbers too, including quantities captured on the battlefield.

Made from bronze, the smooth bore breechloading Napoleons can usually be recognized by a distinctive swell around the muzzle. Confederate production (around 500 in total) varied in style, and many had a simplified outline with no muzzle swell in an attempt to save metal. The southern states also made some in brass and even some from iron, although these needed a reinforcing band around the breech (similar to that used in the Parrott rifles) to reduce the risk of bursting. A few were rifled in later years (see the James rifles entry), although without great success.

James rifles

Charles T. James was a militia general and inventor who attempted to produce bronze rifled weapons, largely by converting existing smoothbore guns such as the Model 1841 6-pounder and even some Model 1857 Napoleons. Some were also made as new guns. The lack of brittleness that made bronze so successful a material for cannons unfortunately also made it too soft to make rifled tubes out of, and the grooves quickly wore out in use.

Parrott rifles

Robert Parrott had served in the army before becoming superintendent of the West Point foundry in New York in 1836. Here he experimented with cast iron as material for guns. At first glance this material appeared to be ideal, being easily available, strong enough to make lighter guns, and hard enough to have rifled tubes.

But it was also brittle, and iron guns had a disturbing tendency to shatter when firing, with no prior warning and usually with fatal results for the gun crew. Parrott attempted to get around this by reinforcing the breech with a wrought iron band around the outside. This reinforcing band was applied while white hot, and the gun rotated as it cooled, causing it to clamp securely all the way around the breech.

Parrott's first gun was rifled piece of 2.9-in bore, designated the Model 1861 10-Pounder Rifle. These Parrott rifles were just in time to take part in the first

These unlucky men have been equipped with the mistrusted 10-pounder Parrott rifle. Effective enough as a weapon, its reputation for bursting without warning made it unpopular with the troops. But as the Parrott was available, that is what they got. The picture also shows how the limbers and caissons were deployed behind the guns, and gives an impression of the numbers of men and horses necessary to move, supply and operate a battery of light artillery.

actions of the war, and many ended up being used by both sides. The Model 1861 was lighter than the Napoleon cannon, extremely accurate at over 2,000 yards, and still effective at 3,000 yards. Mounted on a light carriage, it served both as a field gun and as a defensive piece in static fortifications. Unfortunately, while Parrott's design had strengthened the breech, this just shifted the problem, and his guns quickly developed a reputation for often bursting near the centre, without warning. But they were available, and when intact worked well enough, so continued to be used in large numbers. But their crews never trusted them.

Later Parrott rifles included a 3.67-in 20-pounder, a 30-pounder, the much larger 100-pounder, the 8-inch rifle (200-pounder in army service; 150-pounder with the navy) and the huge 10-inch (army 300-pounder, navy 250-pounder).

The Confederacy made their own copies of Parrott rifles, especially those made by John Mercer Brooke.

3-in Ordnance Rifle

Designed by John Griffen and made by the Phoenix Iron Company, Phoenixville, Pennsylvania, the 3-in Ordnance Rifle became one of the best artillery pieces of its time. Griffen pioneered a new method of welding together layers of wrought iron rods and wrapping them around a cylindrical iron mandrel, then drilling it out and rifling it to form a strong, tough gun tube that was almost unburstable. The new gun was lighter than the Parrott, effective at almost the same ranges (1,900 yards) and almost as accurate as the imported British breechloaders. Low weight made it extremely mobile and popular with horse artillery

Left: A fine study of a 3-in Ordnance Rifle and its fully equipped carriage. Light, strong and with longer range than its smoothbore predecessors, the Ordnance Rifle was popular with its crews. As more Federal batteries became equipped with this rifle, they contributed to the outgunning of Confederate artillery as the war drew to a close.

units, but with over 1,000 made, 3-in rifles were issued as widely as possible to field batteries too. The Confederate States never acquired the technology to make this weapon, and their copies were poor imitations. A superb piece of equipment, it served until the late 1880s, and was only superseded by the advent of reliable steel breechloaders.

British rifled guns

As with their infantry arms, the Confederacy looked abroad, and especially to Britain, for sources of modern artillery equipment. Only small numbers of guns were delivered, partly owing to cost and partly owing to the difficulties of running ships past the Union blockades. And as with small arms, designers rejected by their own government managed to sell their products to an American customer anxious to quickly build up their strength.

One such was Captain Theophilus Blakely, who sold small numbers of rifled breechloaders tot the Confederacy, one of which was delivered in time to take part in the shelling of Fort Sumter in April 1861.

At the end of the war, this Federal soldier guards a captured Confederate 12-pounder Whitworth Rifle. A precision weapon accurate at longer ranges than any other gun, the Whitworth turned out to be fragile and unable to withstand tough combat use in the war. However this steel breechloader was an extremely advanced design that set a marker for the future of artillery after the war.

Other British types were the advanced 3-inch Armstrong rifles, steel breechloaders and accurate to more than 4,000 yards, and the Whitworth rifles. The Whitworths were used in both 2.17-in (6-pounder) and 2.75-in (12-pounder) calibers and used an unusual barrel section, where the tube had an interior hexagonal section which twisted along its length. Whitworth projectiles had flat side faces or facets, angled so they rested against the flat sides of the barrel, and which imparted a spin to the shell when fired. The system was superbly accurate, even out to extreme ranges of 10,000 yards or so, but the breech system didn't stand up well to the harsh treatment of combat operations, and in the end some guns had them fixed shut and the guns loaded via the muzzle.

Mortars

Mortars were a whole sub-class of artillery piece, with extremely short, stubby barrels firing large projectiles at high angles and short ranges. They didn't need much of a powder charge, and their heavy projectiles could destroy most fortifications or throw out a larger spray of heavy fragments than the shell of an equivalent gun.

Mortars could be fired from concealed positions or behind cover, and could drop their shells onto the target even if it were behind obstacles such as hills, buildings or fortified defenses.

The most famous mortar of the war, "The Dictator," was mounted on a railroad flatcar to take part in the siege of Petersburg, Virginia. It needed to be on rails, as at 17,000 pounds it wasn't going to be easily moved any other way. The mortar fired 13-inch projectiles weighing some 225 pounds which could wreck fortress walls and the best prepared dugouts ("bomb-proofs"). A few of these projectiles can be seen at the front of its carriage.

The smallest mortars, known as Coehorns after their inventor (Baron van Coehorn) could be carried into position by two men, were made in both 12- and 24-pounder calibers. Most were made from bronze, although the Confederates made some in iron.

Larger mortars were transported by rail or sea, had calibers of around 8 or 10 inches, and were usually made from iron. The largest were very heavy beasts, initially intended for coastal defense and the protection of waterways. Some were mounted on ship, barges or even on railroad flatcars, and were to used to drop heavy shells onto defensive works and shelters in static siege operations. Such mortars were usually iron, and could have calibers as large as 10 or 13 inches.

The Gatling gun

Rapid firing guns are not thought of as artillery today, but at the time of the Civil War were handled in much the same way, being carried into action on horse-drawn wheeled carriages. Dr Richard Gatling

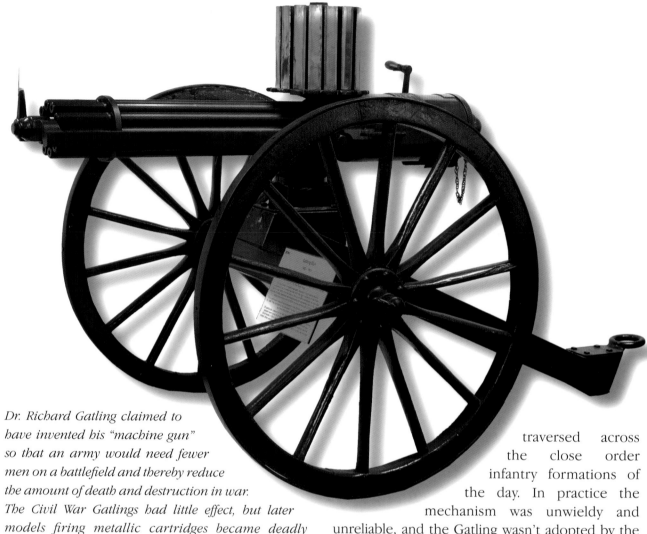

Dr. Richard Gatling claimed to have invented his "machine gun" so that an army would need fewer men on a battlefield and thereby reduce the amount of death and destruction in war. The Civil War Gatlings had little effect, but later models firing metallic cartridges became deadly effective killers. They didn't seem to make warfare any less brutal though. The one shown here was actually made in England to Gatling's patent.

invented the best known of these, although only a few served in the war. Not a true machine gun (it relied on a source of external power) it is nevertheless regarded as the predecessor of the weapons that came to dominate the battlefields of the early twentieth century.

The early six-barreled Gatling fired paper .58 cartridges, which had to first be loaded into a metal sleeve, together with a percussion cap. When the crank handle was turned, each barrel would rotate into place as one of these sleeves was fed into its breech, ready for the firing mechanism to set of the percussion cap. The idea was that the gun could shoot a continuous spray of fire, which could be

traversed across the close order infantry formations of the day. In practice the mechanism was unwieldy and unreliable, and the Gatling wasn't adopted by the government, and those that saw wartime service were private purchases. Gatling later modified the weapon to fire metallic rimfire cartridges, and after the war the revised Gatling went on to great success, both in the United States and overseas.

There were other multi-shot guns that saw service in the war, including the Vandenburgh Volley Gun and crank-operated designs such as the Confederate Williams gun and the Union Agar or "Coffee Mill" gun. None were particularly successful.

Dahlgren guns

Admiral John Dahlgren developed a series of guns from 1850 onwards, initially for use on the navy's small boats operating near the coast and in river estuaries. But the guns were so effective they ended

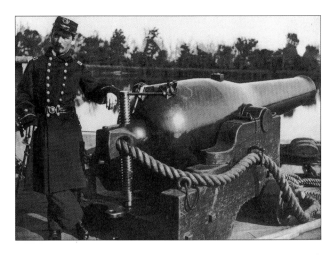

Dahlgren guns were used extensively on ships on both sides, and took part in most of the naval battles of the war. The one shown here illustrates the elevation screw, the restraining ropes and the smooth bottle-like contours of these iron guns.

up on most naval vessels during the war. They included bronze howitzers, iron smoothbore and iron rifled guns. Sizes ranged from 12-pounders to massive 15-inch guns, and the larger weapons were recognisable by their smooth bottle-shaped outline.

Heavy guns

Often referred to as "Columbiads", these were extremely large guns firing heavy projectiles, often at high angles and short ranges. Normally mounted in fortifications covering coastal approaches to harbors and towns, or the larger inland waterways, their sizes ranged up to 15-inch, and some could fire projectiles up to 255 pounds in weight. They were normally made from very thick iron, and most were smoothbore, although a few were rifled. An improved version of the Columbiad type was developed by Lt. Thomas Rodman, who devised a more effective casting method which made for a safer gun able to take more powerful charges. The Confederacy made their own Columbiads, some with reinforcing bands around the breech. But in the end very few of these heavy guns saw much action.

A Confederate copy of a huge Rodman gun sits at Dutch Gap Canal, James River, Virginia. Note how the elevation slots cut into the back of the gun allow it to be moved through a wide vertical angle.

CHAPTER FIVE

Swords and Edged Weapons

"We had been furnished with sabres before we left Abingdon, but the only real use I ever heard of their being put to was to hold a piece of meat over a fire for frying. I dragged one through the first year of the war, but when I became a commander, I discarded it."

Col. John S. Mosby

In a war where the rifled long-arm and explosive shell came to dominate the battlefield, it is ironic that so much effort was put into manufacturing and providing weapons that were anachronistic, obsolete and of limited value. But both sides continued to make thousands of swords for all kinds or purposes, and to supply every rifleman with a bayonet. Their battle usefulness can be demonstrated in the oft-quoted statistic, where Union hospital records show that only half of one percent of all wounds were caused by sword or bayonet.

The only fighting men that had any real use for a combat sword were the cavalry, although even they saw their pre-war visions of massed charges largely disappear in the face of rifle and artillery fire. Instead, much of their battlefield role became that of mounted infantry, dismounting to fire their carbines from the ground. But occasionally they still did come to saber point, and one well-known clash is illustrated by the Don Troiani painting overleaf.

In the infantry, however, only officers and NCOs were entitled to wear a sword. The latter soon left theirs behind as a useless encumbrance,

General William French and his staff pose for a typical "team photograph." Most are carrying Model 1850 Staff and Field Officers swords, intended as a badge of rank rather than a useful military tool.

but the officers kept theirs, more as a badge of rank than as a useful weapon. It did help to distinguish commanders in action, and a sword held high could be used to signal direction of movement, instructions to fire or even the location of a rally point in the noise, smoke and confusion of battle.

Senior officers such as majors and above, had their own patterns of sword, again of mainly symbolic importance, while the wealthier could

purchase finely decorated works of art to demonstrate their personal and financial status.

The pre-war Navy had similar obsolete ideas of mass boarding actions being fought, where seaman and officers would wield broad-bladed cutlasses on contested decks. Again, in practice this almost never happened, although a hefty cutlass could be an intimidating tool for Union inspection parties when intercepting vessels suspected of running their blockade of southern ports.

As for the mass of infantry, every soldier had a bayonet for his rifle or musket. Whether a sword or socket type, they were awkward and cumbersome, affecting the balance and aim of the weapon while making loading more difficult. Initially intended to protect infantry formations from cavalry attack, by the start of the war they were then considered offensive weapons for massed charges. In practice this didn't happen particularly often, but a bayonet did give some protection to man with an empty rifle and no time to reload, and perhaps a boost to his morale when advancing forward into a storm of fire.

And the truly anachronistic use of edged weapons is demonstrated by the unfortunate Confederate formations who were issued with pikes before their rifles became available, while the 6th Pennsylvania Cavalry rode off to the wrong

With their unwieldy saber bayonets towering above them, a formation of men are led off behind a drummer tapping out the cadence. Every rifleman was issued with a bayonet, although only a tiny percentage of the war's casualty list were injured by a bayonet attack.

war with their banners fluttering from their spear-like lances. But in the end, the most common use for the soldier's edged weapon was around camp, in the day-to-day tasks of eating, making camp and making whatever small comforts they could. Never mind a sword or bayonet – every soldier needed a knife.

Overleaf: One action where massed cavalry formations did clash in saber-to-saber combat was at Gettysburg, where Brigadier General Wade Hampton led his cavalry brigade in an attempt to outflank the Army of the Potomac, and was intercepted in turn by Union cavalry. In the ensuing melee, Hampton was cut off by Union troopers and had to fight his way out. He was wounded in the action but soon returned to duty and ended the war as Lieutenant General. Hampton is shown wielding a non-regulation double-edged straight sword while his assailant has a Model 1860 Cavalry Saber.

CAVALRY SABERS

Ames Model 1860 Cavalry Saber

The Model 1860 was intended to replace the earlier Mexican War-era Model 1841 cavalry saber. Based on French designs, it was a slightly lighter sword and a little easier to wield on horseback than it's predecessor. The sword had a narrow 35 in blade, only 1 in wide at the hilt, but as with other swords, there were variations between manufacturers. The handgrip was normally of wood wrapped in leather then wound with twisted copper wire, while the guard was a military pattern three-bar made from brass. The swords shown here are plain, regulation Model 1860s, kept in metal scabbards, and made by the Ames Manufacturing Company, the most prolific American manufacturer of edged weapons.

Above, top: This 1860 pattern cavalry saber has no military markings, while the manufacturer's name, "Ames Mfg Co/Chicopee/Mass.", is in fancy scrolled lettering along the blade. It is most likely to have been a private purchase.

Above, lower: A plain unadorned Ames cavalry sword, this one is stamped "U.S./C.E.W./1864." The grip has the original leather wrapping and wire binding.

The Ames company was started in Cabotville, Massachusetts by Nathan P. Ames, and began making swords in 1832. Early Ames swords were marked "N.P. Ames/Cabotville/Mass." After Nathan died in 1847 the company was continued by his brother James, and markings changed to "Ames Mfg. Co." Cabotville was incorporated into the town of Chicopee in 1848, and the markings on Ames swords were further changed to reflect this. The company rapidly became the most important military sword manufacturer in the United States.

Boyle and Gamble Cavalry Saber

Southern manufacturers produced copies of the Model 1860 saber, often with poorer quality materials, and economy measures such as using brass, wood or leather for the scabbards. The officer's Model 1860 saber shown below was made by Boyle and Gamble of Richmond Virginia. Earlier Boyle and Gamble sabers had scabbards with lighter mounting rings that didn't stand up to hard usage. The second model scabbard shown here had strengthened mounts.

Mansfield and Lamb Cavalry Saber

A fine Model 1860 made by Mansfield and Lamb (shown above), of Forrestdale, RI. Mansfield and Lamb were actually textile manufacturers before taking up the production of cavalry sabers during the war. This sword has been well cared for and is in good condition, complete with metal scabbard, although the copper wire winding is missing from the grip.

A studio portrait of a trooper from the 1st District of Columbia Cavalry. He would spend hours training with his Model 1860 Cavalry Saber, although he would get more effective use from the revolver in the leather holster attached to his belt.

Mole and Sons Saber

As with other weapons, the Confederate States imported swords from a variety of sources. Shown above is a British 1853 Pattern cavalry saber made by Robert Mole and Son of Birmingham, England. The brass guard indicates that this sword was part of an order specially made for the Confederate government, one of the many thousands of such sabers that saw service in the war.

Confederate Cavalry Saber

This is another Confederate saber that appears to have been made by Boyle and Gamble, although there is some dispute between collectors as to origin.

Modified Cavalry Saber

An unusual curiosity, the modified weapon shown above appears to have been based on a Model 1860 cavalry saber. A single shot, underhammer percussion pistol barrel has been built into the grip, a design loosely based on an 1864 patent for a revolver/sword combination.

Roby Cavalry Saber

Another Model 1860-pattern sword (above) in excellent condition marked "C.Roby/W.Chelmsford/Mass." Christopher Roby produced swords in Chelmsford for a few years during the war but ceased production and went bankrupt soon after.

Virginia Manufactory 1st Model Saber

The Virginia Manufactory in Richmond, Virginia, provided muskets, swords and bayonets for the state militia from 1798 to its closure in 1821. Production was restarted when the Civil War broke out, until the factory was eventually destroyed in the burning of Richmond in 1865. The pre-war cavalry sabers produced by the manufactory were known for having long, heavy blades with an extremely curved profile. Many sabers of this type were later carried by Confederate cavalrymen, although most were shortened and had their blade narrowed in an attempt to make them easier to handle. The one shown here is the 1st model, although it has been converted by cutting the blade down to 34 in, with the scabbard shortened to match. The spine is marked "4th Va Regt" which indicates it was originally issued to a pre-war cavalry unit.

Virginia Manufactory 2nd Model Saber

Another Virginia Manufactory Saber (shown above right), this time an unmodified, full-size 2nd Model, with a cumbersome 40-in blade which is over 1.5 in thick at the hilt. The handguard is iron, while the scabbard is steel. The saber has the number "1" engraved on the ricasso (the part of the blade nearest to the hilt) which indicates it was issued to a trooper of the 1st Virginia Cavalry.

The Civil War saw the most modern cartridge repeating carbines on the same battlefields as obsolete weapons from earlier historical epochs. The 6th Pennsylvanian Cavalry rode off to war carrying long lances, with their pennants fluttering from the tips.

A full-length Virginia Manufactory 2nd Model Saber

Kenansville Trooper's Saber

A cavalry trooper's saber attributed to the sword works started by Louis Frolich and which produced, swords, sabers, cutlasses and knives during the war.

INFANTRY SWORDS

Boyle and Gamble
NCO Sword and scabbard

The Model 1840 sword was intended for senior NCOs of infantry units. Early war experience proved such swords to be a cumbersome nuisance on the battlefield, and men very quickly learned to leave them behind in exchange for a firearm such as a rifle or privately purchased revolver. However, thousands were made, and even the hard-pressed Confederacy devoted precious resources to the manufacture of their own versions. This Confederate NCO's sword was made by Boyle, Gamble and MacFee of Richmond Virginia.

Collins Model 1850 Foot Officers Sword

A deluxe quality Model 1850 Foot Officers sword (shown above) made by Collins and Co., of Hartford, Connecticut. The blade is finely etched for much of its length, while the metal scabbard has patterned gilt bronze mounts. A sword of this quality would have been a private purchase.

The Model 1850 was intended for infantry officers at company level (captains and lieutenants), and had a 32-in blade with only a slight curve. The hilt was brass, normally covered in shagreen (the leather-like skin from a seal or shark) and wrapped with twisted brass wire.

Solingen Model 1850

Local manufacturers couldn't meet the demands of wartime production, so many U.S. companies imported blades from foreign makers, where they would be mounted with hilts, guards and scabbards. This M1850 Foot Officers sword (above) has a blade made in Solingen, Germany, one of the most important regions for swordmaking in Europe.

MILITIA SWORDS

Californian Militia Sword

Pre-war militia units were equipped by their state or by private purchase, and the sword shown above is typical of the kind used by militia officers. Intended for an officer in the Californian Militia, it was made by W .H. Horstmann and Sons of Philadelphia. A 32-in slightly curved blade sits inside a wooden scabbard covered in shagreen (seal or shark skin) and complete with a leather frog for attaching it to a sword belt. Note the open handguard with the straight front edge, typical of many pre-war designs. When the war broke out and state militia units mustered to the colors, their officers took their outdated, but trusted, weapons with them.

Eagle Head Militia Sword

This straight-bladed sword is another pre-war militia one, but has a more elaborate finish. Fine engravings decorate the 32.5-in blade, scabbard and counterguard, while the pommel is carved in the shape of an eagle's head. Mother of pearl adorns the grip. Such a finely decorated pre-war sword was probably only intended for peacetime and ceremonial use, but many such ended up going to war with their owners.

STAFF AND FIELD OFFICERS SWORDS

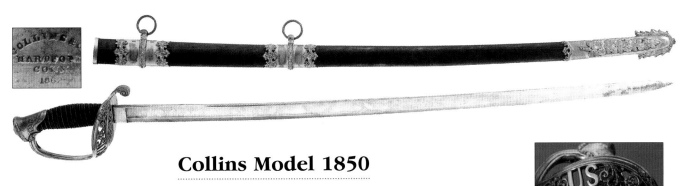

Collins Model 1850

A superb deluxe example of a Model 1850 Staff and Field Officers Sword made by Collins and Co., of Hartford Connecticut. Officers of major and above were authorized to wear swords of this type, and as most were purchased privately, variations in design and level of finish are common. The hilt and scabbard on this one are highly decorated, while the wire-wound grip is covered in shagreen.

Model 1850 Solingen Sword

This staff officers sword shown above has a 33-in blade imported from Solingen, Germany, and is marked "W/Clauberg/Solingen" on the ricasso (the blade root). The blade also has the spread eagle and "U.S." motifs engraved on it, together with fine floral patterns. The guard is of the standard pattern and has been gold-plated. The metal scabbard has a bright finish and decorated brass fittings.

Model 1850 Presentation Swords

Many senior officers swords owned presentation items, given to them by admirers, whether military or civilian, either in thanks for their service or to commemorate particular events. The one shown at the base of the page and right (hilt detail) was presented to Colonel Michael Corcoran on October 11th, 1860, when he led the 69th New York State Militia off to war to take their place alongside the other units of Sherman's brigade.

A close-up of the hilt of Corcoran's fine sword shows the decoration, wire binding and shagreen covering. Corcoran was an Irishman and the decoration has an Irish harp where the "U.S." lettering would normally go.

Above: A finely decorated presentation Staff Officers sword and scabbard, with an engraved 38-in blade from Solingen, Germany. This sword was presented, together with a Smith and Wesson rifle, to Captain Joseph Walker of the 1st New York Engineer Corps from members of his unit. Walker had shown daring bravery and inspiring leadership during the siege of Fort Wagner, South Carolina in the summer of 1863, supervising the digging of saps and siege lines while constantly under fire and in the face of explosive mines (known as "Torpedoes" at the time).

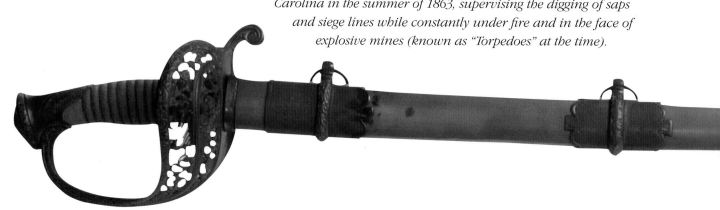

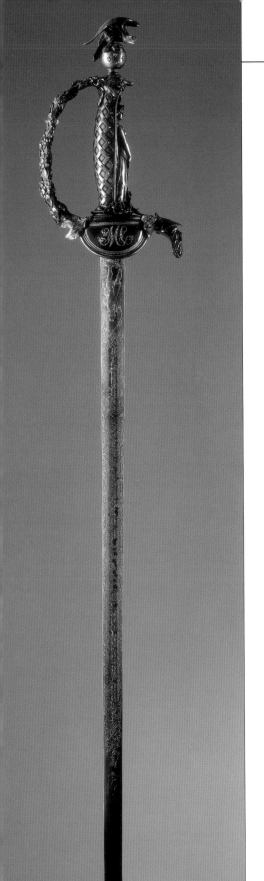

Jeweled Presentation Sword

A splendid jewel-encrusted sword made by Tiffany and Co., New York, and presented to Michael Corcoran (by now a Brigadier General) in January 1863. Corcoran was an Irish immigrant who rose to high command in the war, eventually forming a volunteer brigade which became the core of the renowned Irish brigade. This sword is for commemorative purposes only, it would never have been taken anywhere near a battlefield. See also the previous page for the sword presented to Corcoran while still a Colonel.

Adopting a steely, resolute air, this officer has an infantry pattern sword hanging from his belt.

ARTILLERY SWORDS

Ames Model 1840 Artillery Saber

Before the war, horse artillery units were equipped with the Model 1840 Artillery Saber. A light sword with a 32-in blade, 1.5 in deep at the hilt, it had a pronounced curve in the blade. It was not popular, however, as the curve made it awkward to handle, and many soldiers accused it of being too light to defend against a cavalry saber. Most were discarded after the early months of the war, as artillerymen replaced them with "acquired" Model 1860 Cavalry sabers or with firearms. They continued to be made, however, and the one shown here was produced by N.P. Ames in 1863. The top image shows an officers model, while the lower is a plain trooper's sword with bright finish metal scabbard.

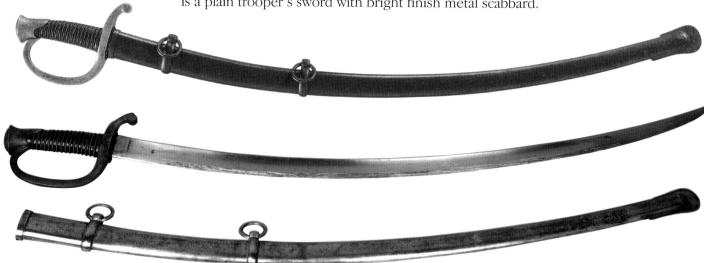

McElroy Artillery Sword

Heavy artillery units were equipped with unusual short, fat swords based on the classical Roman Gladius. The Model 1832 Foot Artillery Sword was typical, with a 19-in blade 1.5 in wide at the hilt, and a simple all-brass hilt with crossbar handguard. Confederate manufacturers made their own copies, such as this one shown below, probably by W.J. McElroy of Macon, Georgia. Note how the blade narrows slightly before the hilt, and the wooden scabbard instead of the more common leather one. It's hard to see what possible combat use a sword of this type would have had.

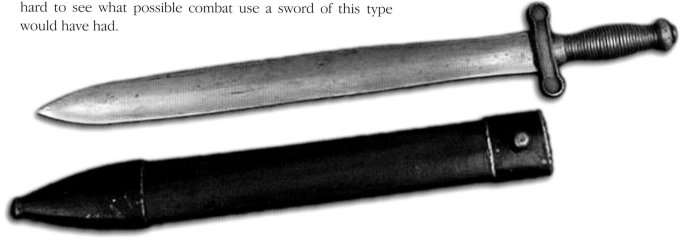

"Star" Artillery Sword

Another Confederate Foot Artillery Sword by an unknown manufacturer. It has the letters "CS" cast into the crossguard and a star in the pommel, a common design known as "CS and Star" style.

NAVAL CUTLASSES

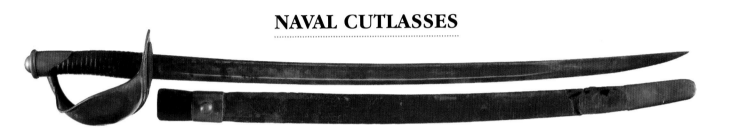

Ames Model 1860 Cutlass

The Model 1860 cutlass (above) entered service just before the war, and resembled the fighting swords issued for land service. This one was made by Ames, and has a wide, slightly curved 26-in blade. The cutlass also has a distinctive wide brass guard and leather-covered wooden grip with brass pommel. The scabbard is leather-covered wood with brass fittings. The officer's version usually had "U.S." or "U.S.N." in the guard. Confederate manufacturers made copies of this cutlass in various styles and finishes.

Confederate Cutlass

In the face of rifled cannon and small arms, the cutlass was obsolete as a naval weapon, but they remained in use throughout the war. The main pre-war design was the Model 1841 (above), with a short, wide 21-in blade and straight crossbar guard. Superseded just before the war began, they the Model 1841 remained in widespread use, and was copied in various forms by Confederate manufacturers. This is one such, possibly made by the Union Car Works in Portsmouth, Virginia.

Cook and Brother Cutlass

An unusual Confederate cutlass (above) made by Cook and Brother in New Orleans with a D-shaped handguard and short, wide blade.

BAYONETS

Socket Bayonets

The most common cutting weapon issued to the infantry soldier was the bayonet, and almost every musket, rifle or carbine had provision for one. The socket bayonet saw most widespread use, and a series of patterns were made. The first one we show (above) is a Model 1855, made to fit Model 1855, 1861 and 1863 rifle muskets. The socket fits over the end of the rifle muzzle, with the locking slot fixes it to a mounting lug, while the blade is offset to give room for the rifleman to reload. This style of bayonet has an 18-in triangular blade with three grooves along its length, ostensibly to make it easier to pull the blade back out from the victim's body. The one shown here has an early war scabbard with two rivets attaching it to the curved belt "frog."

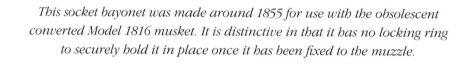

This socket bayonet was made around 1855 for use with the obsolescent converted Model 1816 musket. It is distinctive in that it has no locking ring to securely hold it in place once it has been fixed to the muzzle.

Below: Another triangular bayonet, this time made to fit the Model 1835, 1840 and 1842 muskets.

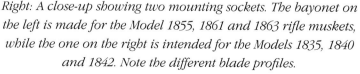

Left: Two close-ups of Model 1855 bayonets and their scabbards. Both scabbards are later Model 1861 types with seven rivets holding the belt frog to the scabbard. The top one is made from bridle leather while the lower is buff leather.

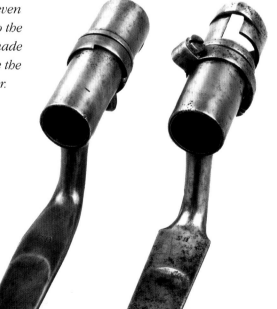

Right: A close-up showing two mounting sockets. The bayonet on the left is made for the Model 1855, 1861 and 1863 rifle muskets, while the one on the right is intended for the Models 1835, 1840 and 1842. Note the different blade profiles.

Saber Bayonets

The other style of bayonet was the sword or saber type, with a more conventional, wide, sword-style blade and handle. Many short rifles were equipped with these. Saber bayonets were even more heavy and cumbersome than socket types, although they did double as useful knives for general camp duties. The Model 1855 was the first U.S. saber bayonet to be produced, and was made for the Model 1855 Rifle.

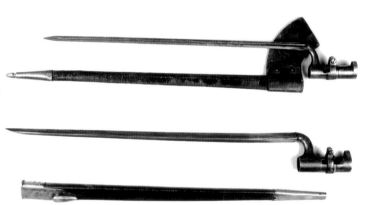

The men and the weapons of the artillery. In front of the 12-pounder "Napoleon", the gunner cradles his Enfield carbine, fitted with its fearsome looking saber bayonet. The officer has a Model 1850 Infantry Officers sword.

Foreign Bayonets

The many foreign rifles that served in the war also had their own bayonets (above). The top one is for the Austrian Model 1854 Lorenz rifle, although the leather scabbard is of American make. The lower one is a socket bayonet for the British P1853 Enfield Rifle, complete with its scabbard. This one is unusual in that the Enfield often came with a large saber bayonet similar to the U.S. Model 1855.

A close-up view (right) of two Austrian Lorenz bayonets. One distinctive aspect of this design is the angled slot for the mounting stud on the rifle barrel. The top one is in the original leather-wrapped wooden scabbard, while the bottom has a U.S. made leather scabbard and two-rivet frog.

OTHER EDGED WEAPONS

Bowie Knife

The edged weapon that was perhaps the most useful to a soldier was the humble knife, and nearly every man equipped himself with one in some form. While a knife was handy as a last-ditch defensive weapon for hand-to-hand combat, its main use was for the myriad of tasks needed to make life bearable on campaign. Cutting branches for shelter and firewood, preparing food, eating, carving domestic items from wood, cutting material for repairs to uniforms – the list is endless.

Large, broad-bladed weapons were the most popular, such as the Bowie knife (at the bottom of the page). It has an 8-in clip point blade and coffin-shaped leather hilt with a brass pommel. The scabbard is also leather.

Pike

The Confederate "Georgia Pike" has passed into Civil War mythology. As the southern armies desperately scoured around for weapons to equip their rapidly forming armies, the State of Georgia ordered some 9,000 pikes to equip some unlucky infantrymen. Notions of massed charges against quivering Union troops who were supposedly "reluctant to face cold steel" backed the purchase of such anachronistic items, although the reality of facing artillery, mass rifled weapons and bayonets would have been very different. Different designs of pikes were produced, including one with a spring-loaded blade. There is no record of any of them actually being used in combat, and most were eventually captured by Sherman's armies.

Confederate Knife

Many different manufacturers made knives, either for military issue, or, more often, for private purchase. This large Bowie-type (shown right) was made for the Confederacy by the Naval Iron Works at Columbus, Georgia. It has an 18-in blade and metal scabbard, which could be attached to a normal sword belt.

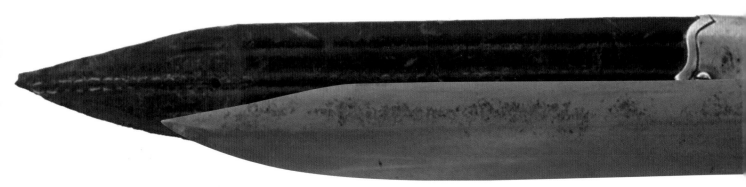